EXPERIEN(

A complete guide to explore the land of diversity

CHRISTEN MORGAN

Table of Contents

Introduction

South Asia is home to the enormous nation of India. With a population of over 1.2 billion, it is the second most populous and seventh-largest country in terms of land area in the entire globe. India is a civic, indigenous democracy with 29 member nations and 7 union houses making up its administrative structure. In addition to being a diverse, multilingual, and multiethnic society, it is also home to a wide range of defended animal habitats. The four main world religions—Hinduism, Buddhism, Jainism, and Sikhism—all have their roots in India. Numerous other religions, including Judaism, Zoroastrianism, slam, and Christianity, are also practiced there. The ancient Indus Valley Civilization, the Vedic civilization, and the Mughal Empire are just a few examples of India's diverse and rich cultural heritage. Indian thrift is the third-largest in the world by purchasing power parity (PPP) and ranks fifth in the world by nominal GDP. Despite having one of the lowest per capita incomes in the world, India is considered a recently industrialized nation. India is a key hub for business process outsourcing, IT-enabled services, and information technology. It is the fourth-largest consumer of motor vehicles worldwide and has one of the fastest expanding automotive industries. With a sizable middle class and quickly developing thriftiness, India is an emerging superpower. It is a significant regional and global power with a substantial military presence. Additionally, India is a member of the World Trade Organization, the G20, the South Asian Association for Regional Cooperation, the Indian Ocean Commission, the G7, and the BRICS alliance. A well-developed network of roads, railroads, airlines, anchorages, and interior aqueducts is part of India's emotional structure, which is well renowned. Several other top-notch metropolises, including Mumbai, Delhi, Bangalore, and Hyderabad, which have emerged as the world's capitals of commerce and assiduity, are also found in India. Rice, wheat, beans, and oilseeds are just a few of the numerous crops grown in India, which is a significant agrarian nation. With some of the most famous landmarks in the world, such as the Taj Mahal, the Golden Temple, and the Ajanta and Ellora grottoes, India is a popular tourist destination. With over 2000 recognized ethnic groups and 22 official languages, India is a country with a unique culture. Numerous public spaces, World Heritage sites, and wildlife sanctuaries can be found there as well. The South Asian Association for Regional Cooperation (SAARC), the G20, and the Commonwealth of Nations all include India as a member. It is a founding member of the Non-Aligned Movement and has close political ties with many nations. India is a significant participant in international politics and frequently hosts guests from other countries. India also contributes significantly to the UN and other international organizations.

Chapter 1: overview on exploring India.

India is an incredibly different country with a rich and fascinating history. From the majestic Himalayas in the north to the stunning strands of the south, India is a country of majestic beauty, rich culture, and vibrant spirit. From the ancient remains of the Indus Valley Civilization to the ultramodern metropolises of the moment, India has a commodity for everyone. India is home to some of the world's most different geographies and societies. From the comeuppance of Rajasthan to the lush tea auditoriums of Darjeeling, India has commodities for everyone. From the bustling cosmopolis of Mumbai, Delhi, and Chennai to the spiritual spots of Varanasi, the Taj Mahal, and Bodh Gaya, India has a commodity to offer everyone. No matter where you go in India, you'll find a unique blend of culture, history, and tradition. India is a great place to explore, as there's a commodity for everyone – whether you 're looking for a comforting sand vacation, a spiritual passage, or an adventure through the jungles of the south. India is also home to some of the world's most amazing wildlife. From barracuda and mammoths in the jungle to the catcalls of the Himalayas, India is a great place to explore the outside. Whether you 're looking for a safari stint or an adventure through the backwoods, India has a commodity for you. India is also a great place to witness the original cuisine. From the racy curries of the south to the tandoori dishes of the north, India has a commodity for everyone. Whether you 're looking for a quick snack or a full-on feast, India has a commodity for you. From the ancient remains of history to the ultramodern metropolises of the present, India is an inconceivable country to explore. Whether you 're looking for an adventure or a comforting vacation, India has a commodity for everyone. With its different geographies, rich culture, and vibrant spirit, India is truly a magical place to explore. India is also home to a variety of persuasions and languages. From the Hinduism of the south to the Buddhism of the north, India is a great place to explore the different faiths of the world. With its blend of ancient traditions and ultramodern culture, India is a great place to learn about different beliefs and societies. With its numerous gutters, timbers, and jungles, India is a great place to explore the outside. Whether you 're looking for a journey in the Himalayas or a comforting voyage down the Ganges, India has a commodity for you. India is also a great place to explore the trades and culture. From the ancient cotillion forms of Kathakali and Bharatanatyam to the ultramodern Bollywood flicks, India has a commodity for everyone. Whether you 're looking for a delightful night out or an artistic experience, India has a commodity for you. India is truly a magical place. With its different geographies, rich history, and vibrant culture, India has a commodity for everyone. Whether you 're looking for a comforting vacation or an adventure, India is a great place to explore. India is a country full of surprises, and the stylish way to explore it's to get out and witness it for yourself.

Historical Development Of India

India has a long and rich history, spanning over 4,500 years. Its ancient culture has been shaped by a number of invasions and migrations from various parts of the world. From the Stone Age to the modern era, India has seen the rise and fall of many powerful empires, which have left their mark on the culture, architecture and politics of the country.

The earliest evidence of human habitation in India dates back to the Stone Age, when the Indus Valley Civilization flourished in the area now known as the modern-day Indian subcontinent. This civilization flourished between 3300 and 1300 BCE, and is credited with having developed one of the world's earliest urban cultures. The Indus Valley Civilization is also credited with having made important contributions to the development of mathematics and the sciences.

After the decline of the Indus Valley Civilization, India witnessed the rise of various other powerful empires. The Mauryan Empire, which was founded by Chandragupta Maurya in the 4th century BCE, was the first great empire of India. This empire was later followed by the Gupta Empire, which ruled for several centuries and is credited with having ushered in a period of great cultural and scientific progress in India.

In the 6th century CE, India was invaded by the Islamic forces of the Arab Caliphate. This invasion marked the beginning of the Muslim rule in India, which lasted until the end of the 18th century. During this period, India was divided into a number of small Muslim kingdoms, and its culture was heavily influenced by the Islamic faith.

The British Raj, which began in the 18th century, marked the beginning of the colonial period in India. The British rule in India lasted until 1947, when India gained independence from the British Empire. Following independence, India adopted a democratic form of government, and has since then seen a period of rapid economic and social development.

Today, India is the world's largest democracy and one of the most rapidly developing countries in the world. Its culture is a unique blend of many different influences, from its ancient roots to the modern influences of the West. India is a country of great diversity, with over 1.2 billion people, who are united by a common language and a common culture.

Since gaining independence, India has become a strong and vibrant democracy, with a rapidly growing economy. It is home to a variety of cultures, languages and religions, and is one of the most diverse nations in the world. India has also made great strides in the fields of science and technology, and is now regarded as a major global player.

The people of India have a proud history of their own, and have made significant contributions to the development of the world. India has a strong sense of national pride and identity, and is currently in the process of building a modern, progressive and prosperous nation. India is also a great example of how a nation can come together despite its differences, and how its people can come together to forge a better future for themselves and for the world.

Geography

India is the seventh- largest country in the world, with an area of square kilometers(square long hauls). It's framed by Pakistan to the northwest, China, Nepal, and Bhutan to the northeast, and Bangladesh and Myanmar to the east. India has numerous physical features, including the Himalayan Mountains, the Thar Desert, and the Indo- Gangetic Plain. The Himalayan Mountains, which run along India's northern border, are the loftiest mountain range in the world, with some of the loftiest peaks in the world. These mountains form a natural hedge between India and the rest of the world, furnishing protection from external pitfalls. The Thar Desert stretches across the western and northwestern corridor of India, and is the 17th largest desert in the world. This desert is substantially thirsty and is a major source of dust storms in the region. The Indo- Gangetic Plain is a veritably rich and densely populated area located in northern India. This plain is formed by the Ganges, Brahmaputra, and Indus gutters and is a major agrarian region. India also has several islets, including the Andaman and Nicobar islets in the Bay of Bengal and the Lakshadweep islets in the Arabian Sea. These islets are home to some of India's most different wildlife, including mammoths, barracuda , and leopards. India's climate varies greatly, from the tropical climate of the south to the temperate climate of the Himalayas. The country also experiences showers, which bring heavy rains to some corridor of the country. India is a veritably geographically different country, with a variety of physical features, climates, and wildlife. The Himalayan Mountains, Thar Desert, and Indo-Gangetic Plain are all part of India's unique terrain, as are its islets and thunderstorm rainfall. Together, these rudiments give a unique and beautiful geography that makes India a great place to visit. India is also home to a variety of ecosystems, ranging from tropical timbers to alpine meadows. The country is also known for its vibrant wildlife, including the Bengal barracuda, Asian giant, Indian rhinoceros, and snow leopard. India has further than 80 public premises and 500 wildlife sanctuaries, furnishing a safe haven for these and other species. India is also blessed with a rich bank. The country has further than 7,500 kilometers of bank, with some of the most beautiful strands in the world. These strands are popular sightseer destinations, and give a great occasion for swimming, sunbathing, and other conditioning. India is a country with a unique geographic identity. Its numerous physical features, climates, and ecosystems make it a fascinating place to explore. The country's wildlife, strands, and public premises give a great occasion to witness the beauty of nature. India is truly a land of unequaled beauty and diversity.

Religion

Religion has been a central part of life in India since ancient times. India is home to four major persuasions Hinduism, Buddhism, Jainism, and Sikhism. These four faiths partake in numerous common beliefs and practices, as well as a rich spiritual and artistic heritage. Hinduism is the oldest and most influential of the four persuasions. It's the maturity religion of India, and rests on the Vedas, a collection of ancient sacred textbooks. Hinduism teaches the generality of Dharma, or righteousness, which is the foundation of all moral and ethical geste. Hindus believe in a Supreme Being, Brahman, who's the source of all life and energy. Buddhism is based on the training of Siddhartha Gautama, the literal Buddha, who lived in India in the 5th century BC. Buddhism stresses the significance of contemplation and awareness in leading a spiritual life. Buddhists believe in the Four Noble verity, the Eightfold Path, and the cycle of birth, death, and rejuvenation. Jainism is an ancient religion that began in India in the 6th century BC. Jains believe in pacifism, respect for all living goods, and the significance of tone-discipline. Jains also believe in air, the law of cause and effect, and the cycle of birth, death, and rejuvenation. Sikhism is a monotheistic religion innovated in the Punjab region of India in the 15th century. Sikhs believe in one God, the training of the ten Sikh Gurus, and the sacred Book, the Guru Granth Sahib. Sikhism emphasizes the significance of service and community, and encourages its followers to lead a life of verity, honesty, and compassion. These four persuasions have shaped and told India's culture, history, and way of life for centuries. moment, the maturity of Indians exercise one of these four persuasions, and millions of people around the world grasp one of them as their own. India is a vibrant and different nation, and its religious heritage is one of its most cherished and celebrated aspects. India is also home to a wide variety of other religious traditions and spiritual practices. These include Islam, Zoroastrianism, and Christianity, which were each introduced to the key by dealers, trimmers, and travelers from other regions of the world. Also, India has a long history of original faiths and ethical persuasions, numerous of which still live. These spiritual practices constantly incorporate rudiments of the four major faiths, as well as rudiments of nature deification and ancestor veneration. Religion plays an important part in Indian society, as it's deeply bedded in the culture and values of the country. For numerous Indians, religious beliefs and practices are integral to their quotidian lives. In India, religion isn't just a set of beliefs and rituals, but a way of life. It's a source of meaning, identity, and belonging, and binds people together in the participated pursuit of spiritual growth and fulfillment.

Language

India is a land of many languages, with more than 18 official languages and thousands of others spoken throughout the country. It is a country of contrasts and a melting pot of cultures and languages that span centuries of history. From the ancient Sanskrit of Hindu hymns to the modern languages of English, Hindi, and Urdu, India's linguistic diversity is one of its most defining characteristics.

The two official languages of India are Hindi and English, while the other official languages are Bengali, Telugu, Marathi, Tamil, Gujarati, Kannada, and Malayalam. Hindi is spoken by the majority of people in India, and is considered the language of official business. English is also widely used in the country and is the language of education in many schools.

The regional languages of India have their own unique histories, cultures, and dialects. These languages are not only spoken in their respective regions, but also form the basis of many regional literary works. For example, Bengali literature is known for its romanticism and vivid imagery, while Marathi literature is known for its poetic style. Other regional languages include Assamese, Punjabi, Oriya, and Kashmiri.

In addition to the official and regional languages, there are also several minority languages spoken in India. These include Nepali, Tulu, Santali, and Mundari. These languages are spoken by small communities of people and have their own distinct history and culture.

India is also home to several dialects, which are variants of the same language. Each dialect is unique to a particular region and is spoken in that area. Some of the most common dialects are Bhojpuri, Maithili, and Konkani.

India is a vibrant country with a rich linguistic and cultural heritage. The many languages of India are a testament to its diversity and a source of pride for its people. From the ancient Sanskrit of Hindu hymns to the modern languages of English, Hindi, and Urdu, India's linguistic diversity is one of its most defining characteristics.

India is home to hundreds of different languages, with numerous of them having their own distinct history and artistic significance. While Hindi is the sanctioned language in India, numerous people also speak a wide variety of other languages. Then's a list of some of the most generally spoken languages in India.

1. Hindi: Hindi is an Indo- Aryan language spoken by further than 260 million people in India, Pakistan, Nepal, and other countries. It's the sanctioned language of India and is one of the 23 sanctioned languages of the country. Hindi is written in the Devanagari script and is the most extensively spoken language in India.

2. English: English is the most extensively spoken language in India after Hindi. It's the language of commerce, government, education, and technology in India. English is spoken by around 125 million people, primarily in the civic areas.

3.Bengali: Bengali is the alternate most extensively spoken language in India, with around 83 million native speakers. It's the language of West Bengal and Tripura countries in India and is written in the Bengali script.

4. Marathi: Marathi is an Indo- Aryan language spoken by around 71 million people in the western and central corridor of India. It's the sanctioned language of Maharashtra and Goa countries in India.

5. Tamil: Tamil is the sanctioned language of Tamil Nadu and Puducherry countries in India. It's also spoken by a large number of people in Sri Lanka, Singapore, and Malaysia. Around 61 million people speak Tamil in India.

6. Telugu: Telugu is the sanctioned language of Andhra Pradesh and Telangana countries in India. It's spoken by around 54 million people in India and is the third most spoken language in India.

7. Gujarati: Gujarati is an Indo- Aryan language spoken by around 46 million people in India, substantially in the countries of Gujarat and Maharashtra. It's the sanctioned language of Gujarat and is written in the Gujarati script.

8. Urdu: Urdu is an Indo- Aryan language spoken by around 41 million people in India. It's the sanctioned language of Jammu and Kashmir and is written in the Nastaliq script.

9. Kannada: Kannada is the sanctioned language of Karnataka and is spoken by around 40 million people in India. It's written in the Kannada script and is the fourth most spoken language in India.

10. Malayalam: Malayalam is the sanctioned language of the state of Kerala in India and is spoken by around 37 million people in India. It's written in the Malayalam script and is one of the oldest languages in India.

11. Punjabi: Punjabi is an Indo- Aryan language spoken by around 29 million people in India and Pakistan. It's the sanctioned language of Punjab state in India and is written in the Gurmukhi script.

12. Oriya: Oriya is an Indo- Aryan language spoken by around 26 million people in India, primarily in the state of Odisha. It's written in the Oriya script and is the sixth most spoken language in India.

13. Assamese: Assamese is the sanctioned language of Assam and is spoken by around 15 million people in India. It's written in the Assamese script and is the seventh most spoken language in India.

14. Kashmiri: Kashmiri is an Indo- Aryan language spoken by around 5 million people in India and Pakistan. It's the sanctioned language of Jammu and Kashmir state in India and is written in the Perso- Arabic script. India is home to a rich diversity of languages and cants, each adding its own unique flavor to the country's culture and heritage. By understanding and embracing the numerous languages of India, we can promote lesser concinnity and understanding between people of different backgrounds.

Climate

India is a large and varied country, stretching from the Himalayas in the north to the tropical beaches of the south. As such, the climate in India is extremely varied, ranging from tropical in the south to temperate and alpine in the Himalayan region.

The northernmost parts of India experience a cold, continental climate, with long, cold winters and short, cool summers, while the central parts of the country experience a temperate climate with hot summers and mild winters, and the southernmost parts of India experience a tropical climate with warm days and nights all year round.

The south-west monsoon season is the main rainy season in India, with most of the country experiencing significant rainfall between June and September. The north-east monsoon season, which brings less rain, occurs between October and December. India also experiences seasonal winds, such as the cold northern wind, known as the "Loo", which blows over the northern plains from April to October.

In the Himalayan region, the climate is much colder, with temperatures often dropping below freezing point in the winter months. This region also experiences heavy snowfall during the winter months, making it an ideal destination for winter sports.

Overall, India has a diverse climate, with each region experiencing its own unique weather conditions and temperatures. The best time to visit

India depends on which region you wish to explore, as each area has its own distinct climate.

India is one of the most different countries in the world, with a wide range of climates and a different terrain. India has an array of climates, ranging from tropical to temperate. India has four main seasons – downtime, summer, thunderstorm and post-monsoon season. Each season brings its own unique rainfall and climate, making India a fascinating place to explore. Then's a list of the different climates set up in India

1. Tropical Wet Climate: This is the most common climate in India, substantially seen in the southern, littoral and eastern corridor of the country. The temperatures are high throughout the time and the moisture is veritably high. This climate is characterized by heavy downfall and hot and sticky rainfall.

2. Tropical Sot Climate: This type of climate is substantially seen in the northern and western corridor of India. The temperatures are high throughout the time with low moisture and veritably little downfall.

3. Tropical Climate: This climate is substantially seen in the hilly regions of India. The temperatures aren't as high as the tropical climates and the downfall is fairly regular throughout the time.

4. Temperate Climate: This type of climate is substantially seen in the northern corridor of India.

The temperatures are cooler than the tropical climates and the downfall is more harmonious throughout the time.

5. Mountain Climate: This is the coldest type of climate in India. It's substantially seen in the mountainous regions and is characterized by veritably cold temperatures and heavy snowfall.

6. Monsoon Climate: This type of climate is substantially seen in the littoral regions of India. Thunderstorm season brings heavy downfall and high moisture. The temperatures generally remain high but they cool down during the thunderstorm season.

7. Desert Climate: This type of climate is substantially seen in the western corridor of India. The temperatures are veritably high with veritably little downfall.

8. Alpine Climate: This type of climate is substantially seen in the advanced mound of the Himalayas. The temperatures are veritably cold and the downfall is low.

9. Mediterranean Climate: This type of climate is substantially seen in the western corridor of India. The temperatures are mild and the downfall is moderate.

10. stickySub-tropical Climate: This type of climate is substantially seen in the central and eastern corridor of India. The temperatures are high throughout the time and the moisture is veritably high.

India is blessed with a wide range of climates, ranging from tropical to temperate. Each climate has its own unique characteristics that make exploring India a great experience. No matter what type of climate you're looking for, you'll be sure to find it in India.

Planning Your Trip

Planning a trip to India can be a daunting task due to its size, diversity, and cultural complexities. However, with some careful planning, you can make your trip to India a memorable one. Here are some tips to help you plan your trip to India.

1. Choose Your Destination: India is a vast country with many amazing destinations. Choose your destination based on your interests, budget, and the time you have. For example, if you are interested in exploring ancient India, you may want to visit Rajasthan. If you are interested in experiencing India's cultural diversity, you can travel to different cities like Delhi, Mumbai, Kolkata, and Chennai.

2. Choose the Right Time of the Year: India's climate varies greatly depending on the region you are visiting. The best time to visit India is usually between October and March when the weather is pleasant and the tourists are fewer.

3. Plan Your Itinerary: Once you have decided on your destination, plan your itinerary. Decide how long you will be staying in each place and make sure to include things like sightseeing, shopping, and activities that interest you.

4. Book Your Travel and Accommodation: Once you have planned your itinerary, book your flights and accommodation. Many online travel sites offer great deals on flights and hotels.

5. Get Vaccinated: Before traveling to India, make sure that you are up to date on all your vaccinations. Depending on which areas of India you are visiting, you may need to get vaccinated against rabies, hepatitis A and B, and typhoid.

6. Get Travel Insurance: Travel insurance is essential for any international trip. Not only does it provide medical coverage, but it also covers you in case of theft or lost luggage.

7. Research the Culture and Language: Research the local culture and language of the region you are visiting. Make sure you know the basics of the local language and customs so that you can communicate effectively with the locals.

8. Bring Cash: It is best to bring cash in the form of rupees with you as some places in India do not accept foreign currency.

9. Stay Safe: Make sure you stay safe while in India by following the local laws and being aware of your surroundings.

10. Pack Light: Since you will be doing a lot of sightseeing, pack light and only bring the essentials. Make sure you bring comfortable shoes as you will be doing a lot of walking.

11. Bring the Right Documentation: Make sure to bring all the necessary documents such as your passport, visas, and other travel documents.

12. Get the Right Gear: Depending on where you are going and the activities you plan to do, make sure to bring the appropriate gear such as a good camera, comfortable clothing, and a good map.

13. Look for Deals: Look for deals on flights, hotels, and other travel related services. Many websites offer great discounts that can help you save money on your trip.

14. Stay Connected: Make sure to stay connected to family and friends while in India by purchasing a local SIM card or a pocket wifi device.

15. Enjoy the Experience: Last but not least, enjoy the experience and all the amazing things India has to offer. Visit the local attractions, explore the local cuisine, and learn about the culture and history.

These are just some tips that can help you plan your trip to India. With proper planning and preparation, you can make your trip to India a memorable one.

Following these tips will ensure that you have a safe and enjoyable trip to India. Don't forget to take lots of pictures and experience all that India has to offer. Have a great trip!

Before You Go

India is a awful country full with a rich tradition and history. Planning a trip to India can be an provocative and satisfying experience, but it's important to make sure that you are properly prepared before you go. also are some tips to help you get ready for your trip to India.

1. Research India: Before you go on your trip, make sure that you do some disquisition on India. Learn about the different regions, the culture and customs, and any implicit safety risks. Get familiar with the language, and be alive of the common scams that you may encounter during your visit.

2. Get Your Documents: In Order Make sure that you have all the necessary documents for your trip. You will need a visa and passport that's up to date. Depending on where you are from, you may also need to get certain vaccinations before you enterthecountry.However, you may need to get an international automobilist's license, If you plan to rent a bus.

3. Prepare Your Wardrobe: India has a lot of different climates, so you will want to make sure that you pack clothes that are applicable for the area that you are visiting. Also, in some areas of India, it's important to dress modestly to show respect for the original culture.

4. Be set For Long Distance Travel: India has a vast network of roads and roads, but they can be truly crowded and uncomfortable. Make sure that you bring some snacks and drinks, and be prepared for long detainments and divergences.

5. Know Your Budget: India is an affordable country to travel in, but you should still plan out your budget in advance so that you can make the ultimate of your capitalist. Make sure that you probe the prices of taverns and lodestones before you go, so that you know how important capitalist you can go to spend.

6. Have emergency Connections: Before you go, make sure that you have the contact information for your original delegation and for any medical services that you may need. It's also a good idea to have the contact information for your family and buddies in case of emergency.

7. Pack for the Heat: India can get truly hot, so make sure to pack light and passable vesture. Sunscreen, hats, and sunglasses are also essential for staying cool and defended from the sun.

8. Research Local Cuisine: India has a variety of succulent, unique dishes, so make sure to do some disquisition before you go. You may want to try some of the original road food, or explore some of the original caffs .

9. Respect Original Customs: India has a rich culture and history, and it's important to show respect for original customs. Learn about the country's form and traditions, and be sure to follow the rules of the original temples and other religious spots.

10. Stay Connected: India has a vast network of mobile phone carriers, so it's easy to stay connected with family and buddies. Make sure to get a original SIM card and a data plan to stay connected while you are in the country. By following these tips and doing your disquisition, you will be sure to have an amazing and safe trip to India. Bon passage!

Getting to India

India is a vast and different country, and getting there can be a bit of a challenge. Still, with a little disquisition and planning, you can make your trip to India an affable and hassle-free experience. Flying to India The most popular way to get to India is by:

Airplane

There are multitudinous international fields in India, the most important being the Indira Gandhi International Airport in Dclhi. International flights from multitudinous countries arrive at this field, including the United States, United Kingdom, Canada, Australia, and more. Other international fields in India include Chhatrapati Shivaji International Airport in Mumbai, Chennai International Airport, and Kolkata International Airport. There are also several indigenous fields that offer international flights from other countries. multitudinous low- cost carriers offer flights to India, so you should be suitable to find a flight that is both accessible and affordable.

Visa

Conditions In order to travel to India, you will need to gain a visa. You can apply for a visa online or at an Indian delegation or consulate in your home country. The visa operation process can take up to 10 days and requires an operation form, passport, passport- sized prints, and possibly other documents analogous as an engagement letter from someone in India.

Arriving in India

When you arrive in India, you will need to complete immigration and customs formalities. You will need to present your passport and visa, and you may need to give substantiation of the onward trip, analogous as a flight ticket. It's important to keep all of your documents safe during your stay in India.

Getting Around India

Once you 're in India, you can use a variety of transportation options to get around. The most popular option is the Indian roads, which offers a reliable, safe, and affordable way to get around the country. Other transportation options include buses , hacks, and domestic flights.

Accommodation

Chancing accommodation in India can be a bit of a challenge, as there is a wide range of options available. Taverns, guesthouses, hostels, and homestays are each popular choices. You can speak your accommodation in advance or find it on appearance. Prices vary depending on the type of accommodation, position, and amenities. Indian cuisine is world- celebrated and is one of the major highlights of a trip to India. There are multitudinous indigenous cuisines to try, so it's a good idea to do some disquisition before you go. multitudinous caffs offer traditional dishes, while road food is a great way to sample original flavors. Be sure to check out original requests as well, as they are a great place to find fresh yield and other particulars.

Safety

India is a safe country to visit, still, it's important to be aware of your surroundings and take introductory safety precautions. Avoid carrying large amounts of cash, keep your valuables safe, and dress modestly in public. It's also a good idea to probe the area you are visiting before you go. Overall, India is an awful destination for travelers . With a little planning and drugs, you can make sure your trip is a success. From the amazing food to the fascinating culture, India offers commodities for everyone. So, what are you staying for? Pack your bags and get ready to explore the cautions of India!

Getting around India

India is a vast and beautiful country with plenty of places to explore. Whether you 're visiting India for a vacation or to witness authentic Indian culture, getting around India can be a challenge. There are multitudinous transport options available and each bone has its own advantages and disadvantages. In order to make the utmost of your trip, it's important to familiarize yourself with the colorful transport options available to you.

By Air:
Flying is the fastest and most accessible way to get around India. There are multitudinous domestic airlines that offer breakouts to major metropolises similar as Delhi, Mumbai, Chennai, Kolkata and other metropolises. You can also fly to some of the lower metropolises like Kochi, Goa, Udaipur and numerous others. Flight prices can be relatively affordable, depending on the airline you choose. The only strike to flying is that it can be relatively precious and there are frequently long ranges at the field.

By Train:
The Indian Railway network is one of the oldest and most expensive in the world. It covers nearly every megacity and city in India and provides a comfortable and affordable way to get around. Trains are generally relatively dependable, although there can be detainments due to rainfall or other issues. You can buy tickets online or at the road station.

By Bus:
Motorcars are one of the most popular forms of transportation in India. motorcars are available in all major metropolises and municipalities, and they

generally give a cheap and comfortable way to get around. You can buy tickets online or at the machine station.

By Auto:

Auto reimbursement is a great option if you 're traveling with a group of musketeers or family. You can rent an auto from the utmost major metropolises and municipalities in India. You'll need to have an International Driving Permit in order to drive in India.

By Taxi:

Taxis are an accessible and dependable way to get around India. You can speak a hack from utmost major metropolises and municipalities. Taxis are also available on apre-paid base, which is generally cheaper than hiring a motorist.

By Rickshaw:

Rickshaws are a common sight in India, and they 're a great way to get around. You can hire a gharry from the utmost major metropolises and municipalities. Cabs are generally relatively cheap and they give an authentic way to witness Indian culture.

By Boat:

India has a vast bank with multitudinous anchorages andharbours.However, also taking a boat could be a great option, If you 're looking to explore the littoral areas of India. Ferries, sails, and other boat services are available in utmost major metropolises and anchorages. Boats give a great way to explore the littoral areas of India in comfort and style.

By Bike:
Also cycling is a great option, If you want to explore India in a further tardy way. You can rent bikes from utmost major metropolises and municipalities in India. This is a great way to explore the original culture and decor at a slower pace.

By Motorcycle:
Also motorcycle hire is a great option, If you 're looking for a further audacious way to get around India. You can rent motorbikes from utmost major metropolises and municipalities in India. Motorcycle hire is generally relatively affordable and offers a great way to explore the country. No matter how you choose to get around India, it's important to be apprehensive of the different transport options available. By familiarizing yourself with the different transport options available, you can ensure that you make the utmost of your trip and get to your destination safely and on time.

Local customs and Humans

India is a vast country with diverse cultural practices, traditions, and customs. Each state and region have their own unique set of customs and beliefs that have been passed down through generations. From food, to festivals, to language, to clothing, India has a variety of local customs and practices that are worth exploring.

1. Food: Indian cuisine is renowned for its flavors and spices. Each region has its own distinct style of cooking, with some areas focusing on specific spices and ingredients. Many of the dishes and recipes have been passed down through generations, and are still eaten by families today.

2. Festivals: The Indian calendar is filled with colorful festivals that are celebrated across the country. From the vibrant Holi festival to Diwali, each festival has its own customs and traditions that are celebrated by local communities.

3. Language: India is home to a variety of languages and dialects, many of which are unique to a particular region. Each language has its own unique set of customs, including greetings, honorifics, and other language-specific customs.

4. Clothing: Clothing is an important aspect of Indian culture, and varies from region to region. From traditional sarees to the distinctive Punjabi suits, there is a range of clothing options that are unique to each region.

5. Weddings: Weddings are a major part of Indian culture and are celebrated with great pomp and show. Each region has its own wedding customs, such as the traditional sangeet ceremony or the exchanging of wedding garlands.

6. Music and Dance: Music and dance are deeply rooted in Indian culture, and each region has its own unique style of music and dance. From the classical dance forms of the North to the folk music of the South, India has a variety of music and dance styles to explore.

7. Greetings: Greetings vary from region to region, with some regions using a handshake or a nod, while others use the traditional Namaste gesture.

8. Religion: India is a diverse country with many religions practiced across its regions. From Hinduism to Islam, each religion has its own set of customs and practices that are followed by its adherents.

9. Arts and Crafts: India is home to a variety of arts and crafts practices that are unique to each region. From the intricate designs of Madhubani paintings to the colorful fabric of Kalamkari, each region has its own distinct style of art and craft.

10. Etiquette: Etiquette is an important part of Indian culture, and varies from region to region. From using the right honorifics to using the appropriate body language, each region has its own set of etiquette that should be followed.

India is a land of diversity and has a vast array of local customs and traditions. Each region has its own unique customs and beliefs and these form an integral part of the culture and heritage of India.

Religion plays an important role in the life of the Indian people and is a major part of the culture. India is a predominantly Hindu country, and Hinduism is the oldest religion in the world. The different religious traditions and beliefs of the local people have resulted in the emergence of various customs and practices.

The Indian people have a deep respect for their elders and the elderly are usually given respect and reverence. This is evident in the way people greet each other or address their elders. Respect for the family is also essential and family ties are cherished.

The Indian people believe in the concept of karma, which is the notion that one's actions in this life will determine one's fate in the next. This is why many Indians are committed to leading a life of good deeds and treating others with kindness and respect.

The caste system is also an integral part of Indian culture. The caste system is a traditional form of social hierarchy and assigns individuals to specific social and economic roles. The caste system has been largely abolished, but it is still practiced in some parts of India, particularly in rural areas.

Indian society is very family-oriented and this is reflected in the way people interact with one another. Indians are very hospitable and enjoy sharing food and spending quality time with family and friends. For this reason, Indians often host large parties and celebrate special occasions with their loved ones.

India is a land of many festivals and celebrations, and each one is unique and special. Festivals such as Diwali and Holi are celebrated with great joy and enthusiasm and are an important part of the local culture.

The Indian people are very passionate about their culture and heritage, and strive to preserve and promote it. Indian culture is a combination of ancient and modern values, and these values are deeply rooted in the hearts and minds of the people. Indian arts and crafts are also an important part of the local culture. From traditional paintings and sculptures to intricate hand-woven fabrics, Indian art is vibrant and full of life. The various musical instruments and styles of music also play an important role in India's culture. India is a country of many languages, and each language has its own unique customs and traditions. India is also home to some of the most ancient and diverse cuisines in the world. Indian cuisine is celebrated all over the world and is characterized by its unique flavors and spices.

Indian people are very proud of their culture and heritage and strive to preserve it. The culture and customs of India are unique and very much a part of the local way of life. It is this unique blend of customs and traditions that makes India such a fascinating country to visit and explore.

Health and Safety in India

Health and safety in India is a major concern due to the country's large population, rapid urbanization and industrialization, as well as the prevalence of poverty and inadequate health care. In addition, India faces a number of unique health and safety challenges due to its geography, climate, and cultural and religious customs.

Poor air quality is a major health and safety issue in India. The air pollution levels in major cities, such as Delhi and Mumbai, are among the worst in the world. Air pollution is caused by a variety of factors, including vehicle emissions, burning of fossil fuels, and burning of biomass, and can lead to increased risk of respiratory and cardiovascular diseases, as well as cancer.

India also has a high rate of occupational health and safety issues due to the lack of enforcement of existing laws and regulations. Many workers in India are exposed to hazardous working conditions, such as poor ventilation, inadequate protective clothing, and exposure to toxic chemicals, which can lead to a variety of health issues, such as respiratory illnesses, skin diseases, and musculoskeletal disorders.

In addition, India has a high rate of accidents and injuries due to unsafe working conditions, inadequate safety regulations, and lack of enforcement. Poor infrastructure and inadequate safety measures can lead to traffic accidents, falls, and other injuries.

India is also susceptible to natural disasters, such as floods, droughts, earthquakes, and cyclones. These disasters can cause significant loss of life and property, as well as disrupt essential services, such as access to clean water and electricity.

The Government of India has taken a number of steps to address health and safety issues in the country. These include the formation of the Ministry of Health and Family Welfare in 2017, the launch of the National Health Policy in 2017, and the launch of the National Health Mission in 2013. The government has also launched several initiatives to improve air quality, such as the National Clean Air Program and the National Clean Air Action Plan.

To address occupational health and safety issues, the government has launched the National Safety Council and has introduced a number of laws and regulations to ensure workplace safety. The government has also taken steps to improve infrastructure and safety measures, such as the Pradhan Mantri Gram Sadak Yojana and the Bharatmala Pariyojana.

Overall, health and safety in India is a major concern, and the government is taking steps to address the issue. However, more needs to be done to ensure that all citizens have access to safe and healthy living and working conditions.

In addition to government initiatives, there are a number of other steps that can be taken to improve health and safety in India. For example, public education campaigns can be used to raise awareness about health and safety issues, such as air pollution, occupational hazards, and natural disasters. Additionally, civil society organizations can work with the government to ensure that laws and regulations are enforced.

Moreover, employers can take steps to ensure that workplaces are safe and healthy for employees, such as providing adequate safety equipment and training and implementing safety protocols. Finally, individuals can take steps to protect their own health and safety, such as wearing protective gear, adhering to safety protocols, and being aware of potential risks.

By taking these steps, India can reduce the number of health and safety issues it faces and ensure that all citizens have access to safe and healthy living and working conditions.

Every Season's Outfit in India

Summer Outfit in India

Summer in India can be brutal - with temperatures soaring to well over 100F! But that doesn't mean you have to sacrifice style for comfort. With the right clothing, you can look stylish and keep cool at the same time. Here are some of the best summer outfit options for India:

Kurtas:

Kurtas are one of the most popular summer outfits in India. They are comfortable and available in a variety of styles and fabrics. Choose a lightweight cotton kurta for a casual look, or opt for more dressy options such as embroidered or embellished kurtas for a more formal look.

Saris:

Saris are a classic style of dress in India, and they are perfect for the summer. Choose a lightweight cotton fabric for a comfortable, yet stylish look. Look for saris with bright, vibrant colors and intricate embroidery or prints for a unique look.

Salwar Kameez:

Salwar kameez is another popular option for summer in India. This outfit consists of a long top and loose pants, and is perfect for a hot day. Choose a lightweight cotton or linen fabric for maximum comfort.

Maxi Dresses:

Maxi dresses are a great option for summer in India. They are comfortable, stylish, and come in a variety of styles and fabrics. Choose a lightweight cotton or linen fabric for a cool and breezy look.

Shorts:

Shorts are a great option for hot days in India. Choose a pair of lightweight, breathable shorts such as denim or linen for a comfortable yet stylish look.

Skirts:

Skirts are also a great option for summer in India. Choose a lightweight cotton or linen fabric for maximum comfort. Look for skirts with bright, vibrant colors and interesting prints for a unique look.

These are some of the best summer outfit options for India. With the right clothing, you can look stylish and keep cool at the same time. So go ahead and pick out your favorite outfit and beat the heat in style!

Jumpsuits:

Jumpsuits are a great way to stay cool during the hot summer months in India. Choose lightweight fabrics such as cotton or linen for maximum comfort. Look for jumpsuits with interesting prints or embellishments for a unique look.

Tunics:

Tunics are also a great option for summer in India. Choose lightweight cotton or linen fabric for maximum comfort. Look for tunics with bright, vibrant colors and interesting prints or embroidery for a unique look.

Linen Shirts:
Linen shirts are a great way to keep cool during the hot summer months in India. Choose lightweight fabrics such as cotton or linen for maximum comfort. Look for linen shirts with bright, vibrant colors and interesting prints or embroidery for a unique look.

Crop Tops:
Crop tops are a great way to stay cool and stylish during the hot summer months in India. Choose lightweight fabrics such as cotton or linen for maximum comfort. Look for crop tops with bright, vibrant colors and interesting prints or embellishments for a unique look.

Sleeveless Blazers:
Sleeveless blazers are a great way to stay cool during the hot summer months in India. Choose lightweight fabrics such as cotton or linen for maximum comfort. Look for blazers with bright, vibrant colors and interesting prints or embroidery for a unique look.

Sandals:
Sandals are a great way to stay cool and comfortable during the hot summer months in India. Choose lightweight fabrics such as leather or canvas for maximum comfort. Look for sandals with bright, vibrant colors and interesting prints or embellishments for a unique look.

Summer:

For the hot and humid summers, Indians prefer light and comfortable fabrics like cottons and linens. The most popular summer attire in India is the Kurta-Pyjama, a long shirt and loose-fitting pyjama. Women can also opt for ethnic sarees and salwar-kameez. Light colors are preferred during this season.

Monsoon:

During the monsoon season, light and airy fabric is preferred to keep cool. Men and women can wear cotton kurtas, lightweight sarees and salwar-kameez. Raincoats and umbrellas are essential accessories during this season.

Winter:

The winter season in India is cold and dry. This is the season for layering clothes. Men can wear woolen sweaters and jackets over a kurta-pajama. Women can wear woolen sarees and salwar-kameez with heavy shawls. Dark colors are preferred for winter clothing.

Festive:

During festival season, most Indians prefer traditional Indian clothes. For men, kurta-pajama and sherwanis are popular. Women can opt for vibrant sarees and salwar-kameez. Bright colors like red, orange and yellow are preferred during this season. No matter what the occasion, Indians love to dress up in traditional clothing. Each season brings its own unique style of clothing and accessories, making it a joy to dress up and look stylish. Regardless of the occasion, Indians love to dress up in traditional attire and accessories that reflect the culture and heritage of the country. Different fabrics, colors, and styles are chosen for different seasons, so that the wearer can look stylish and comfortable. Lightweight fabrics like cotton and linen are preferred for summer, while woolen fabrics are perfect for winter. For monsoon, raincoats and umbrellas are essential accessories. During the festive season, bright colors like red, orange, yellow are preferred. Clothing not only serves the purpose of keeping us warm but also allows us to express our individual style and personality. With traditional outfits, Indians can express their love for the culture and look fashionable at the same time.

Chapter 2: Exploring India.

India is a vast and diverse country, full of ancient culture, stunning landscapes, and vibrant cities. From the majestic Himalayas to the lush tropical forests of the south, India is a country that has something to offer every traveler. Whether you're looking for a spiritual journey, an adventure, or a chance to relax and explore, India is the perfect destination.

If you're looking to explore India's culture, there's no better place to start than the Golden Triangle. This iconic route takes you through Delhi, Agra, and Jaipur, the three most famous cities in India. Here you'll find the stunning Taj Mahal, the beautiful Amer Fort, and the stunning Hawa Mahal. You can also explore the vibrant markets of Delhi, the breathtaking temples of Agra, and the ancient forts of Jaipur.

When it comes to adventure, India is the perfect place. From trekking in the Himalayas to exploring the jungles of Kerala, there are plenty of ways to get your adrenaline pumping. You can also take part in some of India's most popular activities, such as camel safaris and river rafting.

If you're looking to relax and explore, India has something for you too. From the stunning beaches of Goa to the tranquil backwaters of Kerala, there are plenty of places to unwind and take in the beauty of the country. You can also take the time to explore the national parks and wildlife sanctuaries of India.

India is a country of rich diversity, with a wide range of experiences to explore. From the snow-capped peaks of the Himalayas to the stunning beaches of the south, India is a land of beauty and wonder. Home to some of the world's oldest cultures, India offers visitors a unique chance to explore its vibrant cities, ancient monuments, and diverse landscapes. If you're looking to explore India's culture, there's no better place to start than the Golden Triangle. This iconic route takes you through Delhi, Agra, and Jaipur, the three most famous cities in India. Here you'll find the stunning Taj Mahal, the beautiful Amer Fort, and the stunning Hawa Mahal. You can also explore the vibrant markets of Delhi, the breathtaking temples of Agra, and the ancient forts of Jaipur.

When it comes to adventure, India also has plenty to offer. From trekking in the Himalayas to exploring the jungles of Kerala, there are plenty of ways to get your adrenaline pumping. You can also take part in some of India's most popular activities, such as camel safaris and river rafting.

If you're looking to relax and explore, India also has something for you. From the stunning beaches of Goa to the tranquil backwaters of Kerala, there are plenty of places to unwind and take in the beauty of the country. You can also take the time to explore the national parks and wildlife sanctuaries of India.

No matter what type of vacation you're looking for, India is sure to have something to offer. Whether you're looking for a spiritual journey, an adventure, or a chance to relax and explore, India is the perfect destination. So come and explore India – you won't be disappointed!

Top cities in India

Mumbai, Maharashtra

Mumbai, the capital of Maharashtra, is a major metropolitan megacity in India. It's located on the west seacoast of the key and is the largest megacity in India. It's also the fiscal and marketable center of the country. Mumbai is home to further than 20 million people, making it one of the most vibrant metropolises in the world. It's home to numerous sightseer lodestones , including the iconic Gateway of India, Marine Drive, and the Haji Ali Dargah. Mumbai is known for its vibrant culture and escapism. It's a megacity of dreams and the motherland of Bollywood, India's film assiduity. The megacity also has a thriving art, music and theater scene. Mumbai is divided into two corridors, the megacity and the cities. The megacity is home to numerous luxury hospices, cafes, and shopping promenades. The cities are domestic areas with numerous casing options. Mumbai is served by two airfields Chhatrapati Shivaji International Airport and the important lower Juhu Airport. The megacity is also connected to the rest of India by the Mumbai Suburban Railway and the Western and Central Railroads. Mumbai is home to several universities and colleges, including the University of Mumbai, the Indian Institute of Technology Bombay, and the Tata Institute of Social lores. It's also home to several exploration institutions and business seminaries. Mumbai is one of the most popular sightseer destinations in India. It's known for its strands, tabernacles, and monuments. The megacity also hosts several carnivals throughout the time, similar as Ganesh Chaturthi, Diwali, and Holi. Mumbai is a megacity of discrepancy, full of life and energy. It's a megacity of occasion and a place where dreams come true. It's a megacity that nowadays sleeps, and it's a megacity that will always hold a special place in the hearts of its people. Mumbai is also home to numerous major spots such as the Elephanta grottoes, Kanheri grottoes, Mumbai Fort and the Chhatrapati Shivaji Maharaj Vastu Sangrahalaya. It also has a vibrant art scene with the National Gallery of Modern Art, the Chhatrapati Shivaji Maharaj Vastu Sangrahalaya, and the Kala Ghoda Arts Festival. Mumbai is also an important mecca for the Indian business and finance assiduity, with numerous commercial headquarters, banks, and fiscal institutions grounded in the megacity. It's also home to some of India's top business seminaries, including the Indian Institute of Management,

Mumbai. The megacity also has a thriving escapism, with numerous caffs, bars, and clubs. Eventually, Mumbai is home to a variety of religious spots including the Siddhivinayak Temple, the Mahalaxmi Temple, and the ISKCON Temple. Mumbai is a megacity of diversity, culture, and occasion, and is a place that's sure to capture the hearts of all who visit. It's one of India's most instigative metropolises and a must- visit destination for anyone looking to witness the country's vibrant culture.

Attractive facts about Mumbai, Maharashtra

Mumbai is the financial and entertainment capital of India and one of the most vibrant cosmopolis in the world. It's also one of the most attractive cosmopolis in the world, with its bustling expressways, iconic architecture, and different culture. also are some interesting data about Mumbai

1. Mumbai is home to the world's most precious home, Antilla. The 27- bottom structure was erected by the world's fifth-richest person, Mukesh Ambani.

 2. Mumbai is home to the world's largest film industry. It produces more than 1,000 filmlands every time.

3. Mumbai has the topmost number of millionaires and billionaires in India.

4. It's the most vibrant municipality in India, with further than 20 million people living in the metropolitan area.

5. The municipality has a vibrant performance and some of the swish caffs in the country.

6. Mumbai has the world's largest slum, Dharavi.

7. The Gateway of India is a popular corner in Mumbai. It was erected to commemorate the visit of King George V and Queen Mary to India in 1911.

8. Mumbai is home to the world's busiest road station, Chhatrapati Shivaji Maharaj Terminus. 9. The municipality has two World Heritage spots – the Chhatrapati Shivaji Maharaj Terminus and the Elephanta caves.

10. The municipality is home to some of the most iconic mileposts in India, analogous as the Taj Mahal Hotel and Hotel Marine Plaza.

11. Mumbai is also home to some of the swish shopping destinations in the country, analogous as Linking Road, Colaba Causeway, and Fashion Street.

12. The municipality is also home to some of the swish educational institutions in India, analogous as the Indian Institute of Technology(IIT), the University of Mumbai(MU), and the Sydenham College.

13. Mumbai is also home to India's first stock exchange, the Bombay Stock Exchange(BSE).

14. The municipality is home to the largest open-air laundry in Asia, the Dhobi Ghat.

15. Mumbai is home to the world's largest tropical timber, the Sanjay Gandhi National Park.

Where to eat

Mumbai is one of India's most vibrant cities, boasting a wealth of history, culture and of course, tantalizing cuisine. With its wide range of restaurants, there is no shortage of delicious food to try. From the traditional to the modern, from the local to the international, the city's dining scene has something for everyone. Whether you're looking for a quick bite, a romantic dinner, or a luxurious feast, here are some of the best places to eat in Mumbai.

1. The Table: The Table is a chic and modern restaurant located in the heart of Mumbai. With its stylish decor and creative menu, it is one of the city's most popular dining spots. The menu features modern European cuisine, with an emphasis on seasonal ingredients, as well as a selection of wines and cocktails.

2. Indigo: Indigo is a fine-dining restaurant located in Colaba. With its elegant atmosphere and amazing views of the city, it is a great place for a romantic evening. The menu features modern European cuisine, with a focus on seasonal ingredients and classic French techniques.

3. Gajalee: Gajalee is one of the best seafood restaurants in Mumbai. Located in the heart of the city, it is known for its delicious seafood dishes, including seafood curry, prawn masala, and crab masala.

4. Trishna: Trishna is a popular seafood restaurant located in Fort. It is known for its delicious and authentic seafood dishes, including grilled pomfret, lobster masala, and crab curry.

5. The Bombay Canteen: The Bombay Canteen is a modern restaurant located in Lower Parel. With its unique and quirky decor, it is one of the city's hottest dining spots. The menu features a mix of modern Indian and international cuisine, with a focus on local ingredients.

6. Café Mondegar: Café Mondegar is a popular café located in Colaba. It is known for its vibrant atmosphere and amazing selection of food and drinks. The menu features a mix of Indian, Mediterranean, and international dishes, as well as a wide selection of beers and cocktails.

7. Khyber: Khyber is a fine-dining restaurant located in the heart of the city. With its elegant atmosphere and amazing views of the city, it is the perfect place for a romantic dinner. The menu features traditional North Indian cuisine, with a focus on tandoori dishes, as well as a selection of wines and cocktails.

8. Masala Library: Masala Library is a modern Indian restaurant located in the heart of the city. The menu features modern interpretations of classic Indian dishes, as well as a selection of wines and cocktails.

9. Kebab Corner: Kebab Corner is a popular street-food joint located in Bandra. It is known for its delicious kebabs, including shami kebab, tikka kebab, and beef seekh kebab.

10. The Bombay Brasserie: The Bombay Brasserie is a popular restaurant located in the heart of the city. With its elegant atmosphere and amazing views of the city, it is the perfect place for a romantic dinner. The menu features traditional Indian cuisine, with a focus on tandoori dishes, as well as a selection of wines and cocktails.

Where to stay

Mumbai, India's financial capital, is an exciting and vibrant city with a vast array of accommodation options to choose from. Whether you're looking for a luxury hotel, a budget hostel or something in between, there's something to suit every taste and budget. Here's a list of the best places to stay in Mumbai.

1. The Taj Mahal Palace: Set in the heart of Mumbai's Colaba district, The Taj Mahal Palace is one of the city's most iconic hotels. The hotel offers luxurious rooms, excellent dining options and a range of amenities including a spa and pool. The hotel is also home to the iconic Sea Lounge, a popular spot for relaxing with a view of the Gateway of India.

2. The Oberoi, Mumbai: The Oberoi, Mumbai is another luxury hotel in the city. This hotel offers luxurious rooms and suites, as well as a range of amenities including a spa and swimming pool. The hotel also features an array of fine dining options, including the acclaimed Indian restaurant, Vetro.

3. The Leela, Mumbai: The Leela, Mumbai is a luxury hotel located near the airport. The hotel offers luxurious rooms and suites, a range of amenities including a spa and pool, and several excellent restaurants. The hotel also features an outdoor bar and a range of activities and excursions.

4. Novotel, Mumbai: The Novotel, Mumbai is a modern hotel located in the heart of the city. The hotel offers comfortable rooms, a range of amenities and a variety of dining options. The hotel also features a fitness center, swimming pool and a range of other activities.

5. The Orchid, Mumbai: The Orchid, Mumbai is a luxurious hotel located in the heart of the city. The hotel offers luxurious rooms and suites, a range of amenities including a spa and pool, and several excellent restaurants. The hotel also features a bar and an outdoor terrace.

6. The Trident, Mumbai: The Trident, Mumbai is a luxury hotel located in the heart of the city. The hotel offers luxurious rooms and suites, a range of amenities including a spa and pool, and several excellent restaurants. The hotel also features a bar and an outdoor terrace.

7. The Lalit, Mumbai: The Lalit, Mumbai is a luxury hotel located in the heart of the city. The hotel offers luxurious rooms and suites, a range of amenities including a spa and pool, and several excellent restaurants. The hotel also features a bar and an outdoor terrace.

8. The Hyatt Regency, Mumbai: The Hyatt Regency, Mumbai is a luxurious hotel located near the airport. The hotel offers luxurious rooms and suites, a range of amenities including a spa and pool, and several excellent restaurants. The hotel also features an outdoor bar and a range of activities and excursions.

9. The Westin, Mumbai: The Westin, Mumbai is a luxurious hotel located in the heart of the city. The hotel offers luxurious rooms and suites, a range of amenities including a spa and pool, and several excellent restaurants. The hotel also features a bar and an outdoor terrace.

10. The ITC Grand Central, Mumbai: The ITC Grand Central, Mumbai is a luxury hotel located near the airport. The hotel offers luxurious rooms and suites, a range of amenities including a spa and pool, and several excellent restaurants. The hotel also features an outdoor bar and a range of activities and excursions.

Hidden Gems

Mumbai, the capital of Maharashtra, is a bustling metropolis with a vast array of things to do and places to see. While the city is home to some of India's most iconic tourist spots, there are also some hidden gems that are often overlooked. From historical buildings to unique attractions and serene locales, these hidden gems in Mumbai are sure to make your trip even more memorable.

1. The Banganga Tank: This ancient tank is located in the Walkeshwar area of Mumbai and dates back to the 12th century. Built by the Silhara dynasty, the tank is fed by a natural spring and has been a source of water for the locals for centuries. It is surrounded by temples, and is a popular spot for pilgrims and tourists alike.

2. The Asiatic Library: Located in the Fort area of Mumbai, the Asiatic Library is a treasure trove of books, manuscripts, and artifacts from the East

India Company period. It houses a collection of more than two lakh rare books, manuscripts, and maps and is open to the public.

3. Elephanta Caves: Located on Elephanta Island, these caves are around 1000 years old and are a World Heritage Site. The caves are home to several Hindu and Buddhist sculptures, and are a great place to explore the history and culture of the region.

4. Haji Ali Dargah: This 15th century Sufi shrine is located on an island off the coast of Worli in Mumbai. It is one of the most important places of pilgrimage for Muslims in India and is also open to people of all religions.

5. Chor Bazaar: Located in the crowded lanes of South Mumbai, Chor Bazaar is one of the oldest and largest flea markets in India. It is a great place to find unique antiques, handicrafts, and other interesting items.

6. Sanjay Gandhi National Park: Located in the northern part of Mumbai, Sanjay Gandhi National Park is one of the largest parks in India. It is home to several species of plants and animals, and is a great place to explore nature.

7. Kamala Nehru Park: Located near Malabar Hill in South Mumbai, Kamala Nehru Park is a popular spot for joggers and nature lovers. It features a beautiful garden with more than 300 species of trees and plants.

8. Flora Fountain: Located in the heart of South Mumbai, Flora Fountain is a colonial structure built in the 19th century. It is a popular spot for tourists and locals alike and is surrounded by several colonial buildings.

9. Mahim Causeway: Located in the Mahim area of Mumbai, the Mahim Causeway is a popular spot for a stroll. It is a great place to enjoy the breeze from the Arabian Sea and also to take in the views of the Bandra-Worli Sea Link and the Mahim Bay.

10. Film City: Located in the Goregaon area of Mumbai, Film City is a major hub of the Indian film industry. It is a great place to explore the history of Indian cinema and also to catch a glimpse of the stars.

Mumbai is full of hidden gems that are sure to surprise and delight you. From ancient monuments to modern attractions, these hidden gems in Mumbai will make your trip even more memorable. So, plan your next trip to Mumbai and explore these unique attractions!

Beaches and water attractions

Mumbai, the capital of Maharashtra, is home to some of the best beaches and water attractions in India. From the iconic Gateway of India to the stunning beaches of Juhu and Marine Drive, Mumbai is a must-see destination for anyone looking to get away and enjoy the beauty of the sea.

Beaches in Mumbai

1. Juhu Beach: Located on the western coast of Mumbai, Juhu Beach is one of the most popular beaches in the city and a great spot for swimming and sunbathing. It is also home to a variety of street food vendors, making it a great spot to grab a bite to eat after a day at the beach.

2. Girgaum Chowpatty Beach: Another popular beach in Mumbai, Girgaum Chowpatty Beach is a great spot for families, as there are plenty of activities for kids to take part in. From camel rides to kite flying, this beach has it all.

3. Marine Drive: One of the most iconic spots in the city, Marine Drive is a must-visit for anyone who wants to take in the stunning views of the Arabian Sea. It is also a great spot to enjoy a romantic stroll or just sit and enjoy the sunset.

Water Attractions in Mumbai

1. Essel World: Essel World is an amusement park located in Mumbai and is a great spot for families looking for some fun. It offers a variety of rides, games and attractions, making it a great spot to spend a day.

2. Water Kingdom: Water Kingdom is another water-based amusement park located in Mumbai and is a great spot for families and thrill-seekers alike. With a variety of slides, pools and other attractions, there is something for everyone to enjoy.

3. Kartika Water Park: Located in the suburbs of Mumbai, Kartika Water Park is a great spot for families looking for some fun in the sun. With a variety of slides and pools, it is a great spot to spend a day with the family.

4. Madh Island Beach: One of the most popular beach destinations in Mumbai, Madh Island Beach is a great spot for swimming, sunbathing and enjoying the views of the Arabian Sea. It is also home to several restaurants and beach shacks, making it a great spot to grab a bite to eat after a day at the beach.

Mumbai is a great destination for those looking to take in the beauty of the sea and enjoy some of the best beaches and water attractions in India. Whether you're looking for some family fun or a romantic getaway, Mumbai has something for everyone. So grab your swimsuit and your sunscreen, and head to Mumbai for some fun in the sun!

Delhi, Delhi

Delhi, the capital of India, is a bustling and vibrant megacity full of culture and heritage. With a population of over 18 million, it's one of the largest metropolises in the world. Located in the north of India, Delhi is a mecca for trade and commerce, as well as a popular sightseer destination. It's home to some of the most iconic monuments in India similar as the Red Fort, Jama Masjid, and India Gate. Delhi is a megacity of contrasts where old and new attend side by side. It's a megacity of ancient monuments, ultramodern promenades, and bustling requests. The megacity is known for its succulent road food, vibrant escapism, and lively carnivals. Delhi is also a major educational and artistic center, home to numerous prestigious universities and institutes. It's also known for its art and craft, crafts, and traditional jewelry. Delhi has a commodity to offer for everyone. Whether you are looking for a vibrant escapism, artistic guests , or shopping, you will find it in Delhi. No matter what your interests are, you will find a commodity to do in this bustling megacity. Delhi is home to numerous transnational delegations, making it a political mecca. It's also a major transportation mecca, with the Indira Gandhi International Airport and several road stations connecting it to other corridors of India and the world. Delhi also has a rich history, with numerous artistic and religious spots, including the Humayun's Tomb and Qutb Minar. There are also multitudinous premises and auditoriums , making it a great place to relax and decompress. Delhi is a megacity of numerous faces, offering commodities for everyone. Whether you are looking for culture, history, escapism, or just some fun, Delhi is the place to be.

Attractive Facts about Delhi

Delhi – A city of mesmerizing beauty and captivating attractions! Delhi, the capital of India, is a place of great historical significance and is home to a variety of cultures and cuisines. It is one of the most visited cities in the world and is home to some of the most attractive facts in India. Here are some of the most attractive facts about Delhi:

1. Delhi is the world's second-largest city with a population of over 16 million people.

2. Delhi is home to seven World Heritage Sites – Red Fort, Qutub Minar, Humayun's Tomb, Jama Masjid, Old Fort, Jantar Mantar and the Iron Pillar of Delhi.

3. Delhi is one of the greenest cities in India, with 11% of its total area covered by green cover.

4. Delhi is home to a number of historical monuments, including the world-famous Lotus Temple, India Gate and the Red Fort.

5. Delhi is home to some of the best shopping destinations in the world, including Chandni Chowk and Connaught Place.

6. Delhi is home to some of the most delicious street food in India, including chola bhatura, chole kulche, pav bhaji and more.

7. Delhi is home to some of the most vibrant festivals in India, including the International Kite Festival, Diwali and Holi.

8. Delhi is home to one of the oldest universities in the world, the University of Delhi, which was established in 1922.

9. Delhi is home to some of the most renowned museums in India, including the National Museum, National Rail Museum and National Science Centre.

10. Delhi is home to some of the most beautiful parks and gardens, including the Lodhi Garden, Lodi Garden and the Central Park.

These are just some of the most attractive facts about Delhi. From its vibrant culture to its captivating attractions, Delhi is truly a must-visit destination for tourists around the world.

Where to eat

Delhi is home to some of the best food options in India. With a wide range of cuisines and flavors to choose from, it can be hard to decide where to eat in Delhi. Here are some of the top places to get your fill of delicious food in the capital city.

1. Karim's: Located in Old Delhi, Karim's is one of the oldest and most famous restaurants in the city. It serves up traditional Mughlai cuisine such as kebabs and curries, as well as tandoori dishes. The restaurant is renowned for its melt-in-the-mouth kebabs and its generous portions.

2. The Big Chill Cafe: This popular cafe is located in Connaught Place, and serves up a wide range of Italian, Continental, and Mexican dishes. It's a popular spot for those looking for some good comfort food.

3. Chor Bizarre: Located in the heart of the city, Chor Bizarre is a unique restaurant that serves up traditional dishes from the four corners of India. From Kashmiri food to Rajasthani specialties, Chor

Bizarre is the perfect place to sample the flavors of India.

4. Indian Accent: This modern Indian restaurant is located in Lodhi Road and has been named India's best restaurant by the San Pellegrino World Restaurant Awards. It offers a fine dining experience with a unique take on traditional Indian dishes.

5. Bukhara: Located in the Maurya Sheraton Hotel, Bukhara is one of the most popular restaurants in the city. It serves up a range of North Indian dishes, such as tandoori kebabs and curries, along with a few western dishes.

6. Punjabi by Nature: Located in Connaught Place, Punjabi by Nature is a great place to enjoy some traditional Punjabi cuisine. It serves up some of the best Punjabi dishes in the city, such as dal makhani, kadhi, and saag paneer.

7. Imperfecto: Located in Hauz Khas Village, Imperfecto is a great spot for those looking for some Italian and Mediterranean flavors. The restaurant serves up some of the best pizzas, pastas, and salads in the city.

8. Khan Chacha: Located in Khan Market, Khan Chacha is a popular spot for those looking for some delicious street food. It specializes in rolls and kebabs, but also serves up some great North Indian dishes.

9. Parathe Wali Gali: Located in Chandni Chowk, Parathe Wali Gali is the perfect place to get your fill of traditional North Indian food. It serves up some of the best parathas in the city, as well as other North Indian dishes like chole bhature and kulcha.

10. Dhaba by Claridges: Located in Vasant Kunj, Dhaba by Claridges is a great spot to sample some classic North Indian cuisine. It serves up traditional dishes such as dal makhani and kadai paneer, as well as some unique dishes like tandoori jhinga and murgh lababdar.

Where to stay

Delhi is the bustling capital of India and a major rubberneck destination. With its rich history, vibrant culture, and world-notorious lodestones, it's no wonder that Delhi is a popular destination for travelers from around the world.However, there are a number of great choices, If you 're looking for lodging in Delhi. also are some of the swish places to stay in Delhi

1. Taverns: Delhi has a wide selection of taverns, ranging from budget-friendly to luxurious. The municipality has commodity for everyone, from luxury five- star taverns to budget-friendly lodgment. Some popular hotel chains in Delhi include The Taj Mahal Hotel, The Oberoi, and The Hyatt Regency.

2. Hostels: If you 're looking for a more affordable option, hostels are a great choice. hostels are generally less precious than taverns, and they constantly offer amenities analogous as free Wi- Fi, breakfast, and other services. Popular hostels in Delhi include Zostel, Backpacker's Hostel, and Urban Village.

3. Airbnb: Airbnb is a popular accommodation option, especially when traveling to a new city.However, Airbnb can be a great choice, If you 're looking for a cheaper option. Airbnb is also great for those who want to witness the original culture and life of the municipality.

4. Guest Houses: Guest houses are a great option for those looking for a more intimate and unsightly experience. Guest houses are generally run by original families, and they constantly offer a further personalized experience. Popular guest houses in Delhi include Home Stay India, White House Tourist Home, and Heritage Home Inn.

5. Serviced Apartments: Serviced apartments are a great option for those who are looking for a home down from home. These apartments are fully furnished and offer a number of amenities, analogous as Wi- Fi, laundry services, and more. Popular serviced apartments in Delhi include Lemon Tree Premier, The Suryaa, and The Park. No matter where you decide to stay in Delhi, you can be sure that you will have a great time exploring this vibrant municipality. From luxury taverns to budget-friendly hostels, there is a commodity for everyone in Delhi.

Hidden Gems

Delhi is home to a plethora of hidden gems that you can explore and experience. From historical monuments to scenic gardens, Delhi has something to offer everyone. Here is a list of some of the best hidden gems in Delhi:

1. The Garden of Five Senses: This is a beautiful park located near Mehrauli, which is worth a visit for its beautifully landscaped gardens, lush greenery, and a variety of flora and fauna.

2. India Gate: Located in the heart of New Delhi, India Gate is a war memorial dedicated to the soldiers of the Indian army who sacrificed their lives during the First World War.

3. Jama Masjid: One of the largest mosques in India, Jama Masjid is a must-visit for its stunning architecture, intricate carvings, and majestic domes.

4. Lodhi Gardens: Lodhi Gardens is a sprawling park located in the heart of Delhi. It is home to a variety of flora, fauna, and several monuments.

5. National Rail Museum: This museum is a great place to visit for its collection of vintage locomotives, coaches, and photographs.

6. India International Center: The India International Center is one of Delhi's best kept secrets. It is home to a variety of cultural programs and activities, including art exhibitions, film screenings, and book readings.

7. National Museum: The National Museum houses a variety of artifacts from ancient India, including sculptures, coins, manuscripts, and paintings.

8. Qutub Minar: This majestic structure is the highest tower in India, and is a must-visit for its architectural beauty and intricately carved designs.

9. Humayun's Tomb: This 16th century monument is a World Heritage Site and a perfect example of Mughal architecture.

10. Safdarjung Tomb: Located in the heart of Delhi, this stunning mausoleum is a must-visit for its beautiful gardens and intricate carvings.

Beaches and water attractions

Delhi is a bustling metropolis and home to many attractions, including a variety of beaches and water attractions. Whether you are looking for a place to relax and take in the stunning views, or you want to experience some thrilling water activities, there is something for everyone in Delhi.

Beaches:
The Delhi coastline is dotted with pristine beaches, making it the perfect spot for some beachside relaxation. Popular beaches include the Marine Drive Beach, which is located in South Delhi and offers plenty of activities, including beach volleyball, swimming, and sunbathing. The nearby Juhu Beach is also a great spot for swimming and sunbathing, and is home to many street food vendors.

Water Attractions:
Delhi is home to a variety of water attractions, from water parks to boat rides. Adventure Island is a popular water park located in Rohini and has a variety of thrilling water slides. Those looking for a more relaxed experience can take a boat ride along

the River Yamuna, or explore the nearby Delhi Zoo. Other water attractions include the Neela Hauz Lake, which offers a picturesque backdrop for a leisurely stroll, and the Garden of Five Senses, which offers a variety of activities and attractions.

Other Activities:
For those looking to cool off, Delhi offers many other activities. The National Zoological Park of Delhi is a great spot to explore animals and plants, and the nearby Lodhi Gardens is perfect for a leisurely stroll. There are also a number of public swimming pools, including the Talkatora Indoor Stadium and the Delhi University Swimming Pool.
No matter what your preferences are, Delhi has something for everyone. With its stunning beaches, thrilling water attractions, and plenty of other activities, Delhi is a great spot for a relaxing or adventurous holiday.

Bangalore, Karnataka

Bangalore, officially known as Bengaluru, is the capital of the Indian state of Karnataka. It is the largest city in the state and is located in the south-western part of the country. Bangalore is often referred to as the "Silicon Valley of India" because of its reputation as the nation's leading IT hub.

Bangalore is home to many renowned educational and research institutions such as the Indian Institute of Science, Indian Institute of Management Bangalore, National Law School of India University, National Institute of Mental Health and Neurosciences, and the Indian Institute of Astrophysics. In addition to this, it has some of the finest universities in the country such as the University of Mysore, Manipal University, Bangalore University, and Visvesvaraya Technological University.

The city is known for its vibrant nightlife, shopping, and international cuisines. Some of the popular attractions include the Bangalore Palace, Bangalore Aquarium, Lal Bagh Botanical Garden, and Tipu Sultan's Summer Palace. It also has several parks and gardens such as Cubbon Park, Ulsoor Lake, and Lal Bagh.

Bangalore is a major center for IT and BPO industry, contributing to nearly 33% of India's IT exports. Companies like Infosys, Wipro, Accenture, and IBM have their headquarters in the city. The city is also home to many start-ups and provides ample opportunities for new business ideas.

Bangalore is well connected to other cities in the country through air, rail and road. The city is served by Kempegowda International Airport and the Namma Metro Rail.

Overall, Bangalore is an ideal place to live, work and explore. It has a rich cultural heritage, diverse economy and a pleasant climate. It is also an ideal destination for tourists who want to explore the beauty of India.

Attractive Facts about Bangalore Karnataka

Bangalore, the capital of Karnataka, is one of India's most vibrant cities. It is known for its pleasant weather, vibrant nightlife, and diverse culture. The city is also home to some of the most iconic monuments and attractions in the country. From historical sites to modern malls, from ancient temples to sophisticated technology parks, Bangalore has something to offer for everyone. Here are some of the most attractive facts about Bangalore:

1. Bangalore is the IT Capital of India: Bangalore is the IT hub of India and is home to some of the world's biggest IT companies such as Infosys, Wipro, and IBM. It is also the headquarters of the Indian Space Research Organisation (ISRO) and many other top tech firms.

2. Bangalore is a Foodie's Paradise: Bangalore is a paradise for food lovers, boasting over 500 restaurants and eateries. From traditional South Indian delicacies to continental and international cuisines, you can find it all in Bangalore.

3. Bangalore is a Shopping Haven: Bangalore has some of the best shopping malls and markets in the country. UB City, Commercial Street, and Orion Mall are some of the most popular destinations for shopaholics.

4. Bangalore has Beautiful Gardens and Parks: Bangalore is home to some of the most beautiful parks and gardens in India. The famous Lal Bagh, Cubbon Park, and Bannerghatta National Park are some of the most famous attractions in the city.

5. Bangalore is Home to Several Historical Monuments: Bangalore is home to several historical monuments such as Bangalore Fort, Tipu Sultan's Palace, and the Bull Temple. These monuments are a reminder of the city's rich cultural heritage and history.

6. Bangalore is Home to a Thriving Nightlife: Bangalore has a vibrant nightlife, with plenty of pubs, bars, and nightclubs. Some of the most popular nightspots in the city include The Humming Tree, Opus, and Skyye.

7. Bangalore is Home to a Rich Art Scene: Bangalore is home to a rich art scene, with several art galleries, museums, and theatres. The National Gallery of Modern Art and the Karnataka Chitrakala Parishath are some of the most popular places to visit.

8. Bangalore is the Garden City of India: Bangalore is commonly referred to as the garden city of India, due to its large number of parks and gardens. The city is also home to several botanical gardens, including the Lal Bagh and the Cubbon Park.

These are just some of the many attractive facts about Bangalore. From its diverse culture to its vibrant nightlife, there is something for everyone to enjoy in this beautiful city.

Where to eat

Bangalore, India's IT hub, is known for its plethora of fine dining options. With a booming restaurant scene and a variety of cuisines, there's something for everyone in this vibrant city. Whether you're looking for an upscale evening with friends or a casual lunch spot, there are plenty of places to eat in Bangalore. Here are some of the best places to eat in Bangalore.

1. The Only Place: This cozy café serves up authentic North Indian, South Indian, and Continental cuisine. You can enjoy a wide selection of dishes from Chicken Tikka to Kebabs, Curries, and Dosa. The Only Place also offers outdoor seating making it a great spot for a romantic evening.

2. The Fatty Bao: This chic restaurant is known for its Asian fusion dishes such as Sushi, Dim Sum, and Yakitori. The Fatty Bao also has an impressive selection of craft beers and signature cocktails.

3. Masala Library: Masala Library is an upscale restaurant serving modern Indian cuisine. Their menu features unique dishes such as Beetroot Machli, Barley and Quinoa Salad, and Lamb Seekh Kebab. This is the perfect spot for a special occasion dinner.

4. Social: Social is a chain of pubs and bars serving delicious pub food. You can enjoy some of their signature dishes such as Chilli Cheese Fondue, Paneer Tikka, and Chicken 65. Their cocktails and drinks menu is also impressive.

5. Koramangala Social: This trendy bar serves up delicious food, craft beers, and signature cocktails. You can enjoy a wide selection of dishes from appetizers, sandwiches, and pizzas to burgers, kebabs, and pastas.

6. Toit: Toit is a popular microbrewery serving craft beer and delicious pub food. This is the perfect spot for an evening with friends. You can also enjoy some of their signature dishes such as Stuffed Mushroom, Paneer Tikka, and Chicken 65.

7. Barbeque Nation: Barbeque Nation is known for its delicious buffet spread. You can enjoy a wide selection of dishes from North Indian and South Indian to Chinese, Tandoori, and Continental.

8. Smoke House Deli: This chic restaurant serves up delicious dishes such as Pasta, Burgers, Sandwiches, and Pizzas. They also have an impressive selection of craft beers and signature cocktails.

9. Big Pitcher: Big Pitcher is a popular microbrewery serving craft beer and delicious pub food. This is the perfect spot for an evening with friends. They also have a wide selection of cocktails and drinks.

10. The Hole in the Wall Cafe: This cozy café serves up delicious dishes such as Burgers, Sandwiches, and Pizzas. They also have an impressive selection of craft beers and signature cocktails.

These are some of the best places to eat in Bangalore. Whether you're looking for an upscale evening with friends or a casual lunch spot, there are plenty of places to eat in this vibrant city.

Where to stay

Bangalore, Karnataka is a bustling city full of life and culture. With its rich history and vibrant culture, it is no wonder that Bangalore is a popular travel destination for both domestic and international travelers. When it comes to choosing accommodation in Bangalore, travelers have a wide variety of options to choose from. Whether you're looking for a budget-friendly stay or a luxurious option, Bangalore has something to offer you. Here is a list of the best places to stay in Bangalore, Karnataka.

1. Four Seasons Hotel Bengaluru: This five-star hotel is located in the heart of the city and provides luxurious accommodation with modern amenities. Four Seasons Hotel Bengaluru offers an array of services and amenities including a spa, fitness center, swimming pool, and much more.

2. The Oberoi Bangalore: This five-star hotel is located in the city's business district and offers a range of accommodations for both business and leisure travelers. The Oberoi Bangalore offers a range of world-class amenities, including a spa, fitness center, and outdoor pool.

3. The Lalit Ashok Bangalore: This four-star hotel is located in the city center and provides a range of accommodations for both business and leisure travelers. The Lalit Ashok Bangalore offers an array of services and amenities, including a spa, fitness center, and outdoor pool.

4. The Park Bangalore: This five-star hotel is located in the heart of the city and provides luxurious accommodation with modern amenities. The Park Bangalore offers a range of world-class amenities, including a spa, fitness center, and outdoor pool.

5. Grand Mercure Bangalore: This four-star hotel is located near the city's business district and provides a range of accommodations for both business and leisure travelers. Grand Mercure Bangalore offers an array of services and amenities, including a spa, fitness center, and outdoor pool.

6. The Taj Hotel Bangalore: This five-star hotel is located in the heart of the city and provides luxurious accommodation with modern amenities. The Taj Hotel Bangalore offers a range of world-class amenities, including a spa, fitness center, and outdoor pool.

7. The Leela Palace Bangalore: This five-star hotel is located in the city center and provides luxurious accommodation with modern amenities. The Leela Palace Bangalore offers a range of world-class amenities, including a spa, fitness center, and outdoor pool.

8. The Ritz-Carlton Bangalore: This five-star hotel is located in the city center and provides luxurious accommodation with modern amenities. The Ritz-Carlton Bangalore offers a range of world-class amenities, including a spa, fitness center, and outdoor pool.

9. The Gateway Hotel Bangalore: This four-star hotel is located in the city center and provides a range of accommodations for both business and leisure travelers. The Gateway Hotel Bangalore offers an array of services and amenities, including a spa, fitness center, and outdoor pool.

10. Vivanta by Taj Bangalore: This five-star hotel is located near the city's business district and provides luxurious accommodation with modern amenities. Vivanta by Taj Bangalore offers a range of world-class amenities, including a spa, fitness center, and outdoor pool.

Whether you're looking for an affordable stay or a luxurious option, Bangalore has something to offer you. With its rich culture and vibrant atmosphere, Bangalore is a great city to explore and an even better place to stay.

Hidden Gems

Bangalore, Karnataka is a beautiful city filled with hidden gems. From historic sites to lush green gardens and everything in between, there's something for everyone. Here's a list of the top five hidden gems in Bangalore, Karnataka.

1. Tipu Sultan's Summer Palace: Tipu Sultan's Summer Palace is an 18th century architectural masterpiece in the heart of Bangalore. The palace is a unique combination of Indo-Islamic and Gothic styles, and features intricate wooden carvings, a beautiful durbar hall, and a museum dedicated to the life and times of Tipu Sultan.

2. Thottikallu Falls: Located just 25 km from Bangalore, Thottikallu Falls is a great spot for trekking and bird watching. The lush green surroundings make it the perfect spot for a tranquil picnic or a romantic getaway.

3. Nandi Hills: Nandi Hills is a mountain fortress located just 60 km from Bangalore. Its picturesque views and lush green meadows make it a popular destination for trekking and sightseeing.

4. Lal Bagh Botanical Gardens: Lal Bagh Botanical Gardens is a green oasis in Bangalore. It features a variety of flowering plants, trees and shrubs, along with a lake and a glass house. It's a great spot for a romantic stroll or for a family outing.

5. Vidhana Soudha: Vidhana Soudha is the seat of the Karnataka state legislature. Its stunning Neo-Dravidian architecture and sprawling gardens make it a must-visit spot in Bangalore.
These are just a few of the hidden gems in Bangalore, Karnataka. The city has many more to

offer, so if you're looking for a unique experience, be sure to check out some of these hidden gems!

Beaches and water attractions

Bangalore, Karnataka is known for its beautiful beaches and water lodestones. Whether you 're looking for a comforting day at the beach, a thrilling water demesne experience, or a commodity in between, Bangalore has a commodity for everyone. also are some of the swish beaches and water lodestones in Bangalore, Karnataka

1. Jogger's Park Beach: Located in the heart of Bangalore, Jogger's Park Beach offers a serene atmosphere for a day of sunbathing or swimming. The beach is known for its white sand and china clear water, making it the perfect spot for a comforting day.

2. Ulsoor Lake: Ulsoor Lake is one of the most popular lakes in Bangalore. It's a great spot to enjoy a boat lift, take a range, or just relax. The lake is girdled by beautiful amphitheaters and is a popular spot for picnics.

3. Wonderla: Wonderla is a world- class recreation demesne located in Bangalore. It's full of thrilling lifts, water slides, and more. It also has a variety of cafes and shops to check out.

4. Cubbon Park: Cubbon Park is a sprawling demesne located in the heart of Bangalore. It's a great spot to take a tardy range or go for a jam. The demesne also has a beautiful lake with a boat lift.

5. Lumbini amphitheaters: Lumbini Gardens is a popular water demesne located in Bangalore. It features a wide range of water slides, pools, and other lodestones. The demesne also has a large lake, which is perfect for a comforting boat lift.

6. Sankey Tank: Sankey Tank is a large lake located in Bangalore. It's a popular spot for swimming and boat lifts. The lake is also home to a variety of migratory raspberries, making it a great spot for birdwatching. Bangalore, Karnataka is full of beautiful beaches and water lodestones. Whether you 're looking for a comforting day at the beach, a thrilling water demesne experience, or a commodity in between, there's a commodity for everyone in Bangalore.

Chennai, Tamil Nadu

Chennai, the capital city of the Indian state of Tamil Nadu, is known for its rich cultural heritage and vibrant history. Located on the banks of the Bay of Bengal, Chennai is one of the largest cities in India and a major commercial, cultural, and educational hub.

The city is home to many ancient temples, churches, and mosques, and is a popular tourist destination for both domestic and international tourists. Apart from its religious and cultural importance, Chennai is also home to some of India's most advanced industries, including the automobile, information technology, and textiles industries.

The city has a tropical climate and is known for its hot and humid summers and mild winters. The best time to visit Chennai is from November to February, when the temperature is relatively cool, and the city is at its best.

Chennai is also known for its rich cuisine, and visitors can enjoy a variety of delicious dishes, such as dosas, idlis, sambar, and curries. The city is also home to some of the most renowned educational institutions in India, such as the Indian Institute of Technology, Madras, and the Indian Institute of Management, Chennai.

Chennai is also known for its vibrant nightlife and entertainment options, with many bars, pubs, and discos offering a wide range of entertainment. The city is also home to some of India's biggest shopping malls, such as the Phoenix Market City, which offer a variety of fashion and lifestyle products.

Chennai is an exciting and vibrant city, with plenty of things to do and see. Whether you're looking for religious and cultural sites, shopping, or a night out on the town, you'll find everything you need in Chennai.

Attractive facts about Chennai, Tamil Nadu

1. Chennai is the Fourth Largest City in India: Chennai is the fourth largest municipality in India with a population of 8.7 million and is the capital of the state of Tamil Nadu. It's the most vibrant municipality in the south of India and is one of the most visited cosmopolis in the country.

2. Gateway to South India: Chennai is the gateway to South India and is well connected to all major cosmopolis in India. It's also the gateway to the state of Tamil Nadu and provides easy access to the rest of the country.

3. Home to a Vibrant Film Industry: Chennai is home to a vibrant film industry, generally pertaining to Kollywood. It's the second largest film producer in India and has produced some of the most popular and successful films.

4. Ancient temples: Chennai is home to multitudinous ancient temples, including the notorious Kapaleeshwarar temple. The municipality is also home to multitudinous other temples, analogous as the Parthasarathy temple, the Marundeeswarar temple and the Kalikambal temple.

5. Shopping mecca: Chennai is a great shopping destination, offering everything from traditional crafts to modern- day fashion. The municipality is home to numerous shopping malls, road requests and exchange stores. Some of the popular shopping destinations includeT. Nagar, Anna Nagar, Phoenix Market City and Spencer's Plaza.

6. Art and Culture: Chennai is a municipality that is passionate about art and culture. It has numerous art galleries, galleries and theaters that showcase the municipality's rich heritage. The municipality also has multitudinous festivals, analogous as the Madras Music Season, which celebrates classical music and dance.

7. Beaches: Chennai is home to some of the most beautiful beaches in India, analogous as Marina Beach, Elliot's Beach and Covelong Beach. These beaches are perfect for a weekend flight and are popular among locals and sightseers likewise.

8. Cuisine: Chennai is known for its succulent cuisine, which comprises both amenable and non-submissive dishes. The municipality is also home to some of the swish cafes in the country, offering a wide range of cuisines.

9. Technological Hub: Chennai is a mecca for technology and is home to multitudinous software companies, disquisition institutes and IT demesne. The municipality is also a major center for machine manufacturing and is home to multitudinous machine companies.

10. Climate: Chennai has a tropical climate with hot and sticky summers, and mild layoffs. The municipality exploits heavy downfall during the rainstorm months and temperatures range from 20 to 40 degrees Celsius throughout the time.

Where to eat

Chennai, the capital of Tamil Nadu, is known for its succulent traditional South Indian cuisine. The municipality is home to some of the swish caffs cafes and eateries that offer a wide range of cuisines from all corridor of India as well as from around the world. Whether you 're looking for a quick bite or a more relaxed dining experience, there is commodity for everyone in Chennai. also's a list of some of the swish places to eat in Chennai

1. Saravana Bhavan: Saravana Bhavan is a popular chain of amenable cafes that serve authentic South Indian cuisine. It's known for its succulent dosas, idlis and vadas. The café also serves a range of North Indian dishes.

2. Annalakshmi Restaurant: This popular amenable café serves a variety of dishes from all over India. The menu is extensive, with a range of North and South Indian dishes, as well as Chinese and transnational dishes.

3. Buhari: Buhari is one of the oldest cafes in Chennai. It's known for its authentic Chettinad cuisine, which is a blend of traditional Tamil and Muslim flavors. The café has a wide range of dishes, including biryani, kebabs and curries.

4. Ratna Cafe: Ratna Cafe is a popular amenable café that serves a variety of traditional South Indian dishes. The café is known for its dosas, idlis, vadas and other South Indian delectables.

5. Chin Chin: Chin Chin is a popular Chinese café that serves a range of dishes, from dim sum to pates and rice dishes. The café also serves a range of hand dishes.

6. Amethyst: Amethyst is a multi- cookery café that serves a variety of dishes from around the world. The café has a range of international dishes, including Italian, Mexican, Thai and Japanese.

7. Dakshin: Dakshin is a popular South Indian café that serves traditional cuisine from each over India. The café is known for its seafood dishes, as well as its amenable options.

8. Thalappakatti: Thalappakatti is a popular chain of cafes that specialize in biriyani. The café serves a variety of biryani dishes, as well as other traditional South Indian dishes.

9. Chutney's: Chutney is a popular chain of amenable cafes that serves traditional South Indian dishes. The café is known for its succulent dosas, idlis and vadas.

10. Adyar Ananda Bhavan: Adyar Ananda Bhavan is a popular chain of amenable cafes that serve traditional South Indian cuisine. The café is known for its succulent snacks and sweets.

Where to stay

Chennai, the capital of Tamil Nadu, is a bustling city known for its vibrant culture and rich heritage. Boasting a great selection of accommodation, the city has something to offer everyone. Whether you're looking for budget-friendly options, luxurious stays or something in between, here are some of the best places to stay in Chennai.

1. Taj Coromandel:
Located in the heart of the city, the Taj Coromandel is a luxurious 5-star hotel with elegant rooms, fine dining and a variety of leisure activities. It's one of the top places to stay in Chennai if you're looking for a comfortable and opulent experience.

2. Lemon Tree Hotel:
If you're looking for somewhere economical and comfortable, the Lemon Tree Hotel is an excellent option. Located in the bustling Rajiv Gandhi IT Expressway, the hotel offers modern and contemporary rooms, excellent amenities and a host of on-site activities.

3. Vivanta by Taj Connemara:
The Vivanta by Taj Connemara is a 5-star hotel located in the heart of Chennai. Offering luxurious rooms, fine dining, spa services and a range of leisure activities, it's one of the best places to stay in the city.

4. Park Hyatt Chennai:

Park Hyatt Chennai is an upscale 5-star hotel located in the city center. With its luxurious rooms, fine dining, spa services and a range of leisure activities, it's a great option for those looking for a luxurious and comfortable stay.

5. Chennai Residency:

The Chennai Residency is a budget-friendly hotel in the heart of the city. Offering comfortable rooms and excellent amenities, the hotel is an ideal choice for those looking for an economical stay.

6. The Raintree Hotel:

The Raintree Hotel is a great option for those looking for a luxurious stay. Located near the airport, the hotel offers modern rooms, fine dining, spa services and a range of leisure activities.

7. The Gateway Hotel:

The Gateway Hotel is a 4-star hotel located near the beach. With its luxurious rooms, fine dining, spa services and a range of leisure activities, it's the perfect place to stay for those looking for a luxurious and comfortable stay.

8. The Park Chennai:

The Park Chennai is a 5-star hotel located in the heart of the city. Offering stylish rooms, fine dining, spa services and a range of leisure activities, it's the perfect place to stay for those looking for a luxurious and comfortable stay.

9. The Chariot Hotel & Resorts:

If you're looking for somewhere economical and comfortable, The Chariot Hotel & Resorts is an excellent option. Located in the heart of Chennai, the hotel offers modern and contemporary rooms, excellent amenities and a host of on-site activities.

10. The Rain Tree Hotel:

The Rain Tree Hotel is a great option for those looking for a luxurious stay. Located near the airport, the hotel offers modern rooms, fine dining, spa services and a range of leisure activities.

Hidden Gems

Chennai, the bustling capital of Tamil Nadu, is known for its wide variety of attractions ranging from ancient temples to modern malls. But there are also some little-known gems that are worth exploring. From offbeat beaches to little-known art galleries and stunning architectural marvels – Chennai has a lot to offer that many people don't know about. Here is a list of hidden gems in Chennai that you must explore when in the city.

1. Arignar Anna Zoological Park: Spread across 602 hectares, the Arignar Anna Zoological Park is the largest zoological park in India. Located in Vandalur, it is home to a wide variety of animals from around the world, including tigers, lions, giraffes, zebras, and more. The park is also a great place to spot rare species such as the star tortoise and the spotted deer.

2. Semmozhi Poonga: Located in the heart of Chennai, Semmozhi Poonga is a sprawling botanical garden that is home to over 300 species of plants. The park also houses a number of sculptures, fountains, and other attractions, making it a great place to relax and take in the beauty of nature.

3. Pulicat Lake: Located about 60 kilometres from Chennai, Pulicat Lake is the second largest brackish water lake in India. It is home to a wide variety of birds and is a paradise for bird watchers. The lake also offers a range of activities such as kayaking, fishing, and bird watching.

4. Guindy National Park: Spread across 2.82 square kilometres, the Guindy National Park is one of the smallest national parks in India. Located in the heart of Chennai, the park is home to a wide variety of flora and fauna, including rare species such as the blackbuck and the Indian grey mongoose.

5. Arignar Anna Memorial: The Arignar Anna Memorial is a monument dedicated to the memory of the late chief minister of Tamil Nadu, Arignar Anna. The memorial is located in the heart of Chennai and is surrounded by lush greenery. It is a great place to visit to pay your respects to the great leader.

6. Government Museum: The Government Museum is one of the oldest and largest museums in India. Located in Egmore, the museum has a large collection of artefacts and artworks from around the world. It also houses a number of galleries dedicated to natural history, anthropology, and other topics.

7. Vivekananda House: Built in 1897, the Vivekananda House is a memorial dedicated to the great leader and philosopher, Swami Vivekananda. The house is located on the Marina Beach and is a great place to visit if you are interested in learning more about the life and teachings of the great leader.

These are just some of the hidden gems in Chennai that you must explore when in the city. From stunning beaches to ancient monuments, Chennai has a lot to offer. So, don't forget to explore these hidden gems when you are in the city.

Beaches and water attractions

Chennai is a city of wonderful beaches and water attractions. Located on the Coromandel Coast of South India, Chennai is a thriving metropolis with a rich cultural heritage. Home to some of the most spectacular beaches, Chennai has something for everyone. Whether you are looking for a relaxing beach holiday, a thrilling water adventure or a place to watch the sunrise and sunset, Chennai is the perfect place to be. Here is a list of the best beaches and water attractions in Chennai, Tamil Nadu.

Marina Beach: Considered to be the second longest beach in the world, Marina Beach is one of the most popular beaches in Chennai. With soft white sand, sparkling blue waters and a breathtaking view of the Bay of Bengal, Marina Beach is the perfect place to relax and take in the beauty of nature. It is also home to a host of water sports such as kayaking, parasailing, and windsurfing.

Elliott's Beach: Located in south Chennai, Elliott's Beach is a secluded beach with a pristine shoreline. It's a great place to watch the sunrise and sunset, as well as to indulge in swimming and sunbathing. The beach also has a few restaurants where you can enjoy some delicious seafood dishes.

Covelong Beach: Covelong Beach is known for its beautiful coastline and its many water activities. You can go scuba diving, windsurfing, or simply enjoy a relaxing stroll along the shore. There are also several restaurants and beach shacks, where you can enjoy a variety of dishes.

VGP Golden Beach: This beach is a delight for water sports enthusiasts. You can enjoy kitesurfing, kayaking, and swimming in the crystal-clear waters. There are also several shops and restaurants to explore.

Mahabalipuram Beach: Located near the town of Mahabalipuram, this beach is known for its beautiful rock sculptures and temples. You can also enjoy swimming, surfing, and snorkeling in the waters here.

Besant Nagar Beach: Also known as 'Elliot's Beach', Besant Nagar Beach is a popular spot for swimming and sunbathing. There are also several beach shacks, restaurants, and shops to explore.

Kovalam Beach: Located near the city of Kovalam, this beach is known for its tranquil atmosphere and stunning views. You can enjoy a variety of water sports such as parasailing and windsurfing here.

These are just some of the many beaches and water attractions in Chennai, Tamil Nadu. Whether you are looking for a relaxing beach holiday or an exciting water adventure, Chennai is the perfect destination. So, come and explore the beauty of this coastal city!

Must-See Attractions in India

India is one of the most diverse and vibrant countries in the world, with its amazing landscapes and cities, rich culture and heritage, and its multitude of attractions, it's no surprise that millions of tourists visit India every year. From the majestic Himalayas to the majestic beaches of Goa, India is a country full of beauty and adventure.

For those looking to explore India, here is a list of must-see attractions across the country:

1. Taj Mahal – The iconic symbol of love and one of the Seven Wonders of the World, the Taj Mahal is a must-see destination in India. Located in Agra, Uttar Pradesh, the dazzling white marble mausoleum is a stunning example of Mughal architecture and is a World Heritage Site.

2. Golden Temple – Located in Amritsar, Punjab, the Golden Temple is a beautiful and serene place of worship for the Sikh religion. Its architecture is stunning and its peaceful atmosphere makes it a must-see destination in India.

3. Jaisalmer Fort – Located in the Thar Desert in Rajasthan, Jaisalmer Fort is a magnificent sandstone fort that stands tall over the city of Jaisalmer. The fort is a World Heritage Site and a must-see destination in India.

4. Hawa Mahal – Also located in Jaipur, Rajasthan, the Hawa Mahal (Palace of Winds) is an iconic landmark of the city. Its unique red and pink sandstone architecture is a sight to behold.

5. Goa Beaches – Goa is one of the most popular tourist destinations in India, and its beaches are an absolute must-see. From Anjuna to Vagator, Goa's beaches are the perfect place to relax and unwind.

6. Ellora Caves – Located in Maharashtra, the Ellora Caves are an incredible complex of Buddhist, Hindu, and Jain rock-cut temples. The caves are a World Heritage Site and a must-see destination in India.

7. Ajanta Caves – Located in Maharashtra, the Ajanta Caves are a series of 29 Buddhist cave temples. The caves are a World Heritage Site and a must-see destination in India.

8. Kerala Backwaters – Kerala is known as "God's Own Country", and its backwaters are an absolute must-see. Take a boat ride through the tranquil backwaters and admire the stunning scenery of the region.

9. Varanasi – Varanasi is one of the most sacred cities in India, located in Uttar Pradesh. This ancient city is a must-see destination in India, and it's a great place to experience the culture and traditions of the country.

10. Agra Fort – Located in Agra, Uttar Pradesh, the Agra Fort is a stunning red sandstone fort that overlooks the Taj Mahal. It is a World Heritage Site and a must-see destination in India.

India is an incredibly beautiful country, and these are just a few of the must-see attractions it has to offer. From the majestic Taj Mahal to the peaceful backwaters of Kerala, India is sure to provide you with an unforgettable experience.

Off the Beaten Path

India is a beautiful country full of exotic sights and sounds. But if you're looking for something a bit more off the beaten path, here's a list of places you should definitely visit.

1. Zanskar Valley, Jammu and Kashmir: Located in the northwestern part of India, the Zanskar Valley is a stunningly beautiful place. With its snow-capped mountains and breathtaking views, this area is a great place to explore and experience a unique culture.

2. Majuli, Assam: Majuli is the largest river island in the world, located in the Brahmaputra River in Assam. It is home to a variety of cultures, such as the Mishing, Deori, and Sonowal Kacharis. People here still practice traditional crafts like pottery and weaving.

3. Tarkarli, Maharashtra: Tarkarli is one of the most beautiful beach destinations in India. It is known for its crystal-clear waters, white sand beaches, and lush green hills.

4. Bandhavgarh National Park, Madhya Pradesh: Bandhavgarh is a wildlife sanctuary in the central part of India. It is home to a variety of animals, including the Bengal Tiger, leopards, sloth bears, and more.

5. Spiti Valley, Himachal Pradesh: Spiti Valley is a remote area in the Himalayas, located in the state of Himachal Pradesh. It is known for its spectacular views of the Himalayas, ancient Buddhist monasteries, and breathtaking turquoise lakes.

6. Kutch, Gujarat: Kutch is a vast desert region in the state of Gujarat. It is known for its unique culture, stunning salt flats, and colorful markets.

7. Hampi, Karnataka: Hampi is a World Heritage Site and is located in the state of Karnataka. It is known for its ancient temples, rock-cut sculptures, and beautiful landscape.

8. Sunderbans, West Bengal: Sunderbans is a mangrove forest located in the Bay of Bengal. It is home to a variety of wildlife, including the Royal Bengal Tiger.

9. Dhanushkodi, Tamil Nadu: Dhanushkodi is a small village located on the tip of the Rameswaram Island in Tamil Nadu. It is known for its pristine beaches and for being one of the few places in India where the sun rises twice a day.

10. Andaman and Nicobar Islands: The Andaman and Nicobar Islands are located in the Bay of Bengal and are known for their stunning beaches, crystal-clear waters, and lush green forests.

India has so much to offer, and these places are definitely off the beaten path. Whether you're looking for adventure or simply want to escape the hustle and bustle of everyday life, these places are sure to give you an unforgettable experience.

Dining Out in India

Dining out in India is an experience like no other. With a vibrant culture, a dizzying array of flavors and aromas, and a wide array of cuisines, India has something to offer everyone when it comes to dining out. Whether you're looking for a traditional Indian meal or something more adventurous, here's a list of the best places to dine out in India.

1. Hotel Oberoi: Located in New Delhi, Hotel Oberoi is one of the most luxurious dining destinations in India. The restaurant offers a wide range of dishes, including traditional Indian fare and more contemporary international fare. With its elegant decor, incredible service, and delicious food, Hotel Oberoi is a great place to enjoy a fine dining experience.

2. Bukhara: Located in Delhi, Bukhara is one of the most popular restaurants around. The restaurant specializes in North Indian cuisine, with a focus on traditional dishes like kebabs, curries, and tandoori dishes. The restaurant also serves a range of international dishes, making it a great place to try something new.

3. The Taj Mahal Palace: Located in Mumbai, The Taj Mahal Palace is one of the most iconic hotels in India. The hotel's restaurant offers a wide range of dishes, from regional Indian specialties to international dishes. The restaurant also offers a selection of vegetarian dishes, making it a great choice for vegetarians.

4. Indian Accent: Located in Delhi, Indian Accent is one of the most acclaimed restaurants in India. The restaurant serves modern Indian cuisine with a unique spin, making it a great place to experience something new. The restaurant also offers a range of vegetarian dishes, making it a great choice for vegetarians.

5. The Leela Palace: Located in Bangalore, The Leela Palace is one of the most luxurious hotels in India. The hotel's restaurant offers a wide range of dishes, from traditional Indian fare to more contemporary international fare. The restaurant also offers a selection of vegetarian dishes, making it a great choice for vegetarians.

6. Karim's: Located in Delhi, Karim's is one of the most iconic restaurants in India. The restaurant specializes in Mughlai cuisine, with a focus on kebabs and curries. The restaurant also serves a range of international dishes, making it a great place to try something new.

7. Zaffran: Located in Mumbai, Zaffran is one of the most popular restaurants around. The restaurant specializes in North Indian cuisine, with a focus on traditional dishes like kebabs, curries, and tandoori dishes. The restaurant also serves a range of international dishes, making it a great place to try something new. Whether you're looking for a traditional Indian experience or something more adventurous, dining out in India is an experience like no other. With its vibrant culture, dizzying array of flavors and aromas, and wide array of cuisines, India has something to offer everyone when it comes to dining out.

Chapter 3: Activities

India is an expansive and diverse nation that offers something for everyone. With its varied terrain and climate, India has an abundance of activities to explore and enjoy. Whether you're looking for a thrilling adventure, cultural exploration, or simply a relaxing holiday, there is no shortage of activities in India for you to experience.

For those looking for a thrilling adventure, India offers many exciting activities that will get your heart racing. From white water rafting in Rishikesh to paragliding in Manali, there are plenty of opportunities to get your adrenaline pumping. There are also many extreme sports to be explored, such as mountain biking, rock climbing and bungee jumping.

For those who are looking to explore India's culture and history, there are several activities to choose from. You can visit the many historical sites and monuments throughout India, such as the Taj Mahal, Red Fort and Qutub Minar. You can also explore the many temples, ancient ruins, and wildlife reserves found throughout the country.

For those looking for a relaxing holiday, India offers plenty of activities to suit all tastes. Whether you're looking to take part in a yoga or meditation retreat, or simply relax on a beach, there are plenty of options. You can also take part in activities such as cooking classes, safaris, bird watching and more.

No matter what type of activities you're looking for, there is something for everyone in India. From thrilling adventures to relaxing holidays, India has something for everyone. So go ahead and explore the many activities India has to offer.

Shopping

Shopping in India

India is a shopper's paradise, with an array of products, services, and experiences to choose from. India is renowned for its traditional handicrafts, textiles, and jewelry, as well as its modern consumer goods. Whether you are looking for unique souvenirs, special gifts, or something for yourself, India has something for everyone and every budget. Here is some information about shopping in India.

Types of Shopping:

India has a variety of shopping options, ranging from traditional bazaars to modern malls. Traditional bazaars offer an amazing variety of handicrafts, textiles, jewelry, and other traditional items. Most large cities also have modern malls, which offer a wide selection of consumer goods, from clothing to electronics.

Shopping Experiences:
Shopping in India is an experience in itself. The vibrant colors, the bustling markets, and the friendly haggling create a unique atmosphere. Most markets offer a wide variety of items, so you can find something for everyone. Shopping in India is also a great way to interact with the locals, learn about their culture, and get some amazing bargains!

Tips for Shopping in India:
When shopping in India, it's important to keep a few tips in mind. First, haggling is expected, so don't be shy about asking for a lower price. Second, be sure to inspect items carefully, as quality can vary. Third, keep in mind that some items may not be available in your home country, so it's a good idea to take advantage of the opportunity to buy them in India. Finally, don't forget to bargain for the best price!
Shopping in India is an amazing experience, and one that you won't soon forget. Whether you're looking for souvenirs, gifts, or something for yourself, India has something for everyone. With its vibrant markets, friendly people, and great bargains, shopping in India is sure to be an unforgettable experience. So, if you're looking for a unique shopping experience, India is the place to go!

Markets

Requests in India are vibrant and varied, with a wide variety of goods, services and gests available to those who visit. From vibrant stores to ultramodern promenades, India has a commodity to offer for everyone. With a rich and different culture, India is home to a wide variety of requests, ranging from traditional shopping capitals to ultramodern

shopping promenades.

Traditional stores: Traditional Indian stores, or requests, are frequently located in the busiest corridor of the megacity, girdled by bulging thoroughfares and vibrant colors. Then callers will find a variety of goods and services, from traditional Indian apparel and jewelry to spices, fruits and vegetables. numerous of these requests are also home to road food merchandisers, offering an array of succulent dishes to try. Ultramodern Promenades India is home to numerous ultramodern shopping promenades, which offer an array of products, services and guests . These promenades are frequently located in the heart of metropolises and are filled with transnational brands, caffs, playhouses, and entertainment installations similar as brushing alleys and passageways.

Flea Markets: Flea requests are a great way to explore the culture and history of India. They frequently feature a variety of particulars, from relics and crafts to alternate- hand apparel and accessories. numerous of these requests also offer a range of road food, making them a great place to test the original cookery.

Souks: Souks are traditional requests set up in the Middle East and North Africa. India is also home to a number of these vibrant requests, dealing everything from fantastic spices to handwrought jewelry.

Night Markets: Night requests are getting increasingly popular in India, offering an array of goods and services until late into the night. These requests are frequently set up in sightseer areas, furnishing callers with an occasion to explore original culture and experience the escapism. growers ' requests growers ' requests are a great way to support original growers and directors. Then callers will find a variety of locally- grown fruits and vegetables, as well as a selection of manual products and crafts. These are just a few of the numerous requests set up in India. With such a wide variety of goods, services and guests available, it's no wonder why so numerous people flock to India's vibrant requests. Whether you 're looking for traditional particulars or ultramodern guests , India is sure to have a commodity to offer.

Water sports

Water sports in India have grown in popularity in recent years, with many people looking to take advantage of the country's vast coastline, numerous rivers and lakes, and even its mountainous terrain. From sailing to kayaking, scuba diving to surfing, India has something for everyone who loves the water.

Sailing:

Sailing is a popular water sport in India, with plenty of sailing clubs and courses available in the country. From Chennai to Goa, Mumbai to Kochi, sailing is an exciting way to explore the country's coastal waters. There are plenty of sailing races and regattas held throughout the year, giving sailors a chance to show off their skills and compete against each other.

Kayaking:

Kayaking is a great way to explore India's rivers and lakes. From the Ganges River to the Himalayan Lakes, kayakers can paddle through some of the country's most beautiful and remote areas. There are plenty of kayaking clubs and courses available throughout India, offering a range of experiences, from beginner to advanced.

Scuba Diving:

India is blessed with a wealth of marine life and stunning coral reefs, making it a popular destination for scuba divers. From the Lakshadweep Islands to the Andaman and Nicobar Islands, there are plenty of places to explore the underwater world. There are plenty of scuba diving courses and instructors available throughout India, so it's easy to find a course that's suitable for your level of experience.

Surfing:

India is home to some of the best surfing in the world, with waves that are perfect for both beginners and experienced surfers. From Kovalam to Goa, there are plenty of surfing spots to explore. There are plenty of surf schools available throughout India, offering lessons and equipment hire, so it's easy to find the right place to learn how to surf.

Water Skiing:

Water skiing is a great way to explore India's many lakes and rivers. From Kolkata to Bangalore, there are plenty of places to try your hand at water skiing. There are plenty of water skiing clubs and courses available throughout India, offering a range of experiences, from beginner to advanced.

Windsurfing:

Windsurfing is an exciting way to explore India's coastal waters. From the beaches of Kerala to the backwaters of Goa, windsurfing is a great way to experience the country's stunning coastline. There are plenty of windsurfing clubs and courses available throughout India, offering a range of experiences, from beginner to advanced.

Jet Skiing:

Jet skiing is a great way to explore India's many rivers and lakes. From the Ganges River to the Himalayan Lakes, jet skiers can have a thrilling time on the water. There are plenty of jet skiing clubs and courses available throughout India, offering a range of experiences, from beginner to advanced.

These are just some of the many water sports available in India. Whether you're looking for a relaxing cruise or an adrenaline-packed adventure, India has something for everyone who loves the water.

Island hopping

Island hopping in India is an amazing way to explore the country's diverse coastline. From the tranquil beaches of the Andaman and Nicobar Islands to the bustling city-islands of Goa, India has a wide range of islands to explore. Whether you're looking for adventure, relaxation, or cultural immersion, island hopping in India offers something for everyone.

When it comes to island hopping in India, the Andaman and Nicobar Islands are a great place to start. These beautiful islands are located in the Bay of Bengal and are known for their tranquil beaches and stunning coral reefs. There are plenty of activities to keep you busy here including snorkeling, diving, swimming, and fishing. You can also explore the local culture by visiting the villages and interacting with the locals.

Goa is another great place for island hopping in India. There are over 30 islands here, many of which are small and quiet. The most popular islands include Divar, Chorao, and Grande de Vagator. These islands are known for their beautiful beaches, and they also offer plenty of activities like trekking, water sports, and sightseeing. There are also plenty of luxurious resorts and restaurants to choose from.

The Lakshadweep Islands are also a great destination for island hopping in India. Located off the coast of Kerala, these islands are known for their stunning white-sand beaches and crystal-clear waters. Here, you can spend your days snorkeling and diving, or just lounge on the beach and soak up the sun. You can also explore the local culture, or visit the local markets to find some unique souvenirs.

No matter where you decide to go island hopping in India, there are plenty of activities and attractions to keep you busy. From the beautiful beaches of the Andaman and Nicobar Islands to the bustling city-islands of Goa, India has something for everyone. So, pack your bags and get ready to explore the country's diverse coastline!

Art Galleries in India

India is home to a wide variety of art galleries showcasing the country's diverse and vibrant culture. From traditional art to modern, India has something for everyone. Here is a list of some of the best art galleries in India that are worth visiting:

1. National Gallery of Modern Art (NGMA), New Delhi: The NGMA is the premier art gallery in the country, featuring an impressive collection of modern and contemporary Indian art from the 19th century to the present. It also showcases some of the best international works from the early 20th century to the present day.

2. Kashi Art Gallery, Kochi: Located in Kochi, the Kashi Art Gallery is one of the most renowned art galleries in India. It showcases a wide range of contemporary artworks from both Indian and international artists. The gallery also hosts several exhibitions and workshops.

3. Chitrakala Parishad, Bangalore: Located in Bangalore, Chitrakala Parishad is one of the oldest and most respected art galleries in the country. It showcases the best of traditional, modern and contemporary art from both Indian and international artists.

4. Piramal Art Gallery, Mumbai: The Piramal Art Gallery is one of the most respected and well-known galleries in Mumbai. It showcases a wide variety of artworks from both Indian and international artists, ranging from traditional to contemporary art.

5. India Habitat Centre, New Delhi: The India Habitat Centre is home to one of the largest art galleries in India. It showcases some of the best works of modern and contemporary Indian and international art. The gallery also hosts several exhibitions and workshops.

6. Chitra Kala Sangam, Chennai: Located in Chennai, Chitra Kala Sangam is one of the oldest art galleries in India. It showcases some of the best works of traditional and contemporary art from both Indian and international artists.

7. National Museum of India, New Delhi: The National Museum of India is one of the most renowned art galleries in the country. It features an impressive collection of ancient and modern Indian art, as well as works from international artists.

8. Delhi Art Gallery, New Delhi: The Delhi Art Gallery is one of the largest and most respected art galleries in India. It showcases some of the best works of modern, contemporary and traditional art from both Indian and international artists.

9. Academy of Fine Arts, Kolkata: Located in Kolkata, the Academy of Fine Arts is one of the most renowned art galleries in India. It has a large collection of traditional and contemporary Indian art, as well as works from international artists.

10. Tao Art Gallery, Mumbai: The Tao Art Gallery is one of the most respected and well-known galleries in Mumbai. It showcases a wide variety of artworks from both Indian and international artists, ranging from traditional to contemporary art.

Nice Parks and Garden

India is home to some of the most beautiful parks and gardens in the world. From the lush green forests of the Himalayas to the vibrant flora of the Western Ghats, India offers a wide range of outdoor spaces for outdoor activities and relaxation. Here is a list of some of the most beautiful parks and gardens in India.

1. Mughal Gardens, Kashmir: Mughal Gardens in Kashmir are one of the most beautiful parks in India. It is surrounded by tall Chinar trees and the gardens are filled with a variety of flowers, shrubs and trees. This park is a great place to take a leisurely stroll or just to relax and admire the beauty of nature.

2. Langkawi Island National Park, Malaysia:
Langkawi Island National Park is a beautiful park located on the Malay Peninsula. It is home to some of the most exotic wildlife and plants. The park also offers a variety of activities such as trekking, mountain biking and bird watching.

3. Botanical Garden, Kolkata: The Botanical Garden in Kolkata is a must visit for nature lovers. It is home to a variety of plants and trees from different parts of the world. It is also home to the world's largest Banyan tree.

4. Sanjay Gandhi National Park, Mumbai: Sanjay Gandhi National Park is a natural reserve located in Mumbai. The park is home to a variety of wildlife and plants. It is also home to the world's largest butterfly sanctuary.

5. The Corbett National Park, Uttarakhand: The Corbett National Park is located in Uttarakhand and is home to a variety of wildlife and plants. It is also home to tigers, leopards and elephants.

6. Lal Bagh Botanical Gardens, Bangalore: Lal Bagh Botanical Gardens in Bangalore is one of the most beautiful parks in India. It is home to a variety of plants and trees and offers a variety of activities such as bird watching, trekking and picnicking.

7. Valley of Flowers, Uttarakhand: The Valley of Flowers in Uttarakhand is home to a variety of wildflowers and plants. It is a great place to take a leisurely stroll and admire the beauty of nature.

8. The Jog Falls, Karnataka: The Jog Falls in Karnataka is one of the most spectacular waterfalls in India. It is a great place to take a leisurely stroll and admire the beauty of nature.

9. Indian Botanical Garden, Kolkata: The Indian Botanical Garden in Kolkata is India's oldest botanical garden. It is home to a variety of plants and trees and offers a great place to relax and admire the beauty of nature.

10. The Rock Garden, Chandigarh: The Rock Garden in Chandigarh is a great place to visit. It is home to a variety of rocks and sculptures and provides a great place to take a leisurely stroll and admire the beauty of nature.

11. The Nalabana Island, Bihar: The Nalabana Island in Bihar is one of the most beautiful parks in India. It is home to a variety of wildlife and plants and provides a great place to relax and admire the beauty of nature.

12. Lodi Gardens, Delhi: The Lodi Gardens in Delhi is one of the most beautiful parks in India. It is home to a variety of flora and fauna and offers a great place to relax and admire the beauty of nature.

13. The Sunderbans National Park, West Bengal: The Sunderbans National Park in West Bengal is home to a variety of wildlife and plants. It is also home to the Royal Bengal Tiger and provides a great place to take a leisurely stroll and admire the beauty of nature.

14. The Hanging Gardens, Mumbai: The Hanging Gardens in Mumbai is one of the most beautiful parks in India. It is home to a variety of plants and trees and offers a great place to relax and admire the beauty of nature.

15. The Garhwal Himalayas: The Garhwal Himalayas is home to a variety of wildlife and plants. It is also home to some of the highest peaks in the world and provides a great place to take a leisurely stroll and admire the beauty of nature.

These are just some of the most beautiful parks and gardens in India. India is a great place for nature lovers and these parks and gardens offer a great getaway from the hustle and bustle of city life. So, make sure to visit some of these parks and gardens on your next trip to India.

Restaurant and Relaxation Areas

Caffs and Relaxation Areas in India India is a vibrant country with an array of societies and cookeries. From the majestic Himalayas to the bustling metropolises, India has commodity for every rubberneck. For savorers, India is full of succulent caffs and relaxation areas. There's a comprehensive list of the stylish caffs and relaxation areas in India.

1. The Oberoi Grand, Kolkata: The Oberoi Grand is a five- star hostel located in Kolkata, India. It's one of the oldest hospices in India and is famed for its majesty and substance. The hostel has a variety of caffs, each offering a unique dining experience. The caffs serve a range of transnational cookery and indigenous specialties. In addition to its caffs, the hostel has a gym, swimming pool and a fitness center, making it the perfect spot for relaxation and revivification.

2. The Park, Mumbai: The Park is a popular luxury hostel located in Mumbai. It's famed for its vibrant escapism and exquisite dining options. The hostel has a variety of caffs, each offering a unique culinary experience. The caffs serve a range of dishes from Indian, Chinese and European cookery. In addition to its caffs, the hostel also has a gym, swimming pool and a fitness center, making it the ideal spot for relaxation and revivification.

3. The Taj Mahal Hotel, New Delhi: The Taj Mahal Hotel is a major hostel located in New Delhi. It's famed for its beautiful armature, luxurious amenities and exquisite dining options. The hostel has several caffs, each offering a unique dining experience. The caffs serve a range of transnational and indigenous dishes. In addition to its caffs, the hostel also has a gym, swimming pool and a fitness center, making it the perfect spot for relaxation and revivification.

4. The Leela Palace, Udaipur: The Leela Palace is an iconic hostel in Udaipur, India. It's famed for its majesty and substance. The hostel has a variety of caffs, each offering a unique dining experience. The caffs serve a range of dishes from Indian, Chinese and European cukery. In addition to its caffs, the hostel has a gym, swimming pool and a fitness center, making it the ideal spot for relaxation and revivification.

5. The Vivanta by Taj, Goa: The Vivanta by Taj is a luxurious hostel located in Goa, India. It's famed for its vibrant escapism and exquisite dining options. The hostel has a variety of caffs, each offering a unique dining experience. The cafes serve a range of dishes from Indian, Chinese and European cookery. In addition to its caffs , the hostel also has a gym, swimming pool and a fitness center, making it the perfect spot for relaxation and revivification.

6. The Lalit, New Delhi: The Lalit is a luxurious hostel located in New Delhi. It's famed for its majesty and substance. The hostel has a variety of caffs, each offering a unique dining experience. The caffs serve a range of dishes from Indian, Chinese and European cookery. In addition to its caffs, the hostel also has a gym, swimming pool and a fitness center, making it the perfect spot for relaxation and revivification.

7. The Taj Lands End, Mumbai: The Taj Lands End is a popular luxury hostel located in Mumbai. It's famed for its vibrant escapism and exquisite dining options. The hostel has a variety of caffs, each offering a unique culinary experience. The caffs serve a range of dishes from Indian, Chinese and European cookeries. In addition to its caffs, the hostel also has a gym, swimming pool and a fitness center, making it the ideal spot for relaxation and revivification.

8. The Grand Hyatt, Goa: The Grand Hyatt is a luxurious hostel located in Goa, India. It's famed for its vibrant escapism and exquisite dining options. The hostel has a variety of caffs, each offering a unique culinary experience. The caffs serve a range of dishes from Indian, Chinese and European cookery. In addition to its caffs, the hostel also has a gym, swimming pool and a fitness center, making it the perfect spot for relaxation and revivification.

9. The Oberoi Amarvilas, Agra: The Oberoi Amarvilas is a five- star hostel located in Agra, India. It's famed for its majesty and substance. The hostel has a variety of caffs, each offering a unique dining experience. The caffs serve a range of transnational cookery and indigenous specialties. In addition to its caffs. The hostel also has a gym, swimming pool and a fitness center, making it the ideal spot for relaxation and revivification.

10. The Taj Lake Palace, Udaipur: The Taj Lake Palace is a luxurious hostel located in Udaipur, India. It's famed for its majesty and substance. The hostel has a variety of caffs, each offering a unique dining experience. The caffs serve a range of dishes from Indian, Chinese and European cukery. In addition to its caffs, the hostel also has a gym, swimming pool and a fitness center, making it the perfect spot for relaxation and revivification. These are just some of the stylish cafes and relaxation areas in India. Whether you 're looking for a lavish regale or a comforting gym, India has a commodity for everyone. So go ahead and explore the caffs and relaxation areas of India and make the utmost of your holiday.

Top Hindu's Temple in India

India is known for its religious and spiritual heritage, and its many temples are a testament to this fact. Hinduism is one of the oldest and most popular religions in the world, and it is practiced by millions of people in India. The country is home to some of the most important and sacred Hindu temples in the world, and these places of worship attract visitors from all over the world. Here is a list of the top Hindu temples in India that are worth visiting.

1. Tirupati Balaji Temple – This temple is located in the state of Andhra Pradesh and is dedicated to Lord Venkateswara, a reincarnation of Lord Vishnu. It is considered to be one of the most important pilgrimage sites in India and is visited by millions of devotees every year.

2. Jagannath Temple – This temple is located in the state of Odisha and is dedicated to Lord Jagannath, a form of Lord Vishnu. It is one of the most important pilgrimage sites in the country and is visited by millions of devotees from all over the world.

3. Somnath Temple – This temple is located in the state of Gujarat and is dedicated to Lord Shiva. It is believed to be one of the twelve jyotirlingas in India and is considered to be one of the most important pilgrimage sites in the country.

4. Vaishno Devi Temple – This temple is located in the state of Jammu and Kashmir and is dedicated to the Hindu goddess Vaishno Devi. It is one of the most important pilgrimage sites in the country and is visited by millions of devotees from all over the world.

5. Golden Temple – This temple is located in the state of Punjab and is dedicated to Lord Guru Nanak. It is one of the most important Sikh pilgrimage sites in the country and is visited by millions of devotees from all over the world.

6. Meenakshi Temple – This temple is located in the state of Tamil Nadu and is dedicated to Goddess Parvati. It is one of the most important pilgrimage sites in the country and is visited by millions of devotees from all over the world.

7. Ranganathaswamy Temple – This temple is located in the state of Tamil Nadu and is dedicated to Lord Ranganatha, a form of Lord Vishnu. It is one of the most important pilgrimage sites in the country and is visited by millions of devotees from all over the world.

8. Kashi Vishwanath Temple – This temple is located in the state of Uttar Pradesh and is dedicated to Lord Shiva. It is one of the most important pilgrimage sites in the country and is visited by millions of devotees from all over the world.

9. Kamakhya Temple – This temple is located in the state of Assam and is dedicated to Goddess Kamakhya. It is one of the most important pilgrimage sites in the country and is visited by millions of devotees from all over the world.

10. Konark Sun Temple – This temple is located in the state of Odisha and is dedicated to the Sun God. It is one of the most important pilgrimage sites in the country and is visited by millions of devotees from all over the world.

Top Churches in India

There are several cultures, traditions, and faiths in India. With so many different religions, India has a large number of sacred sites, temples, and churches. The top churches in India are shown below out of all the churches there.

1. The Basilica of Bom Jesus in Goa: Located in Goa, the Basilica of Bom Jesus is the oldest church in India. It was constructed in 1594 and is named for St. Francis Xavier. A World Heritage Site, the church is renowned for its exquisite Baroque design.

2. San Thome Basilica in Chennai: This church can be found in Chennai. St. Thomas, one of the twelve apostles of Jesus Christ, is honored by this 16th-century structure, which bears his name. The church, a well-liked destination for pilgrimages, is renowned for its exquisite Gothic architecture.

3. Cathedral of St. Thomas in Kottayam: Located in Kottayam, Kerala, the Cathedral of St. Thomas is one of the country's oldest cathedrals. It was constructed in 1599 and has St. Thomas, one of Jesus Christ's twelve apostles, as its patron saint. The church is a well-liked destination for pilgrims and is renowned for its exquisite architecture.

4. Kolkata's St. Paul's Cathedral: Located in Kolkata, the St. Paul's Cathedral is one of India's most recognizable cathedrals. It was constructed in 1847 and has St. Paul as its dedication. The church, a well-liked destination for pilgrimages, is renowned for its exquisite Gothic architecture.

5. Fort Kochi's St. Mary's Church: The St. Mary's Church is one of India's oldest churches and is situated there. It honors the Virgin Mary and was constructed in 1516. The church, a well-liked destination for pilgrimages, is renowned for its exquisite Gothic architecture.

6. The Sacred Heart Cathedral in Delhi: Delhi is home to the Sacred Heart Cathedral, one of India's most well-known cathedrals. It is devoted to the Sacred Heart of Jesus and was constructed in 1931. The church, a well-liked destination for pilgrimages, is renowned for its exquisite Gothic architecture.

7. St. Andrew's Church in Bandra: Located in Mumbai's Bandra neighborhood, the St. Andrew's Church is one of the country's most well-known churches. It is dedicated to St. Andrew and was constructed in 1838. The church, a well-liked destination for pilgrimages, is renowned for its exquisite Gothic architecture.These churches rank among India's most well-liked ones. These churches each have a distinctive architectural style and history. These churches are certain to provide you an amazing experience, whether you're seeking a religious or architectural encounter.

Top mosques in India

India is home to many of the most beautiful and remarkable mosques in the world. From the iconic Taj Mahal to the intricate Jama Masjid, India has some of the most breathtaking examples of Islamic architecture. Many of these mosques have been around for centuries and have become symbols of India's rich cultural and religious heritage. Here is a list of some of the most impressive mosques in India.

1. Jama Masjid, Delhi: This grand mosque, located in Delhi, is one of the largest and most impressive mosques in India. Built in 1656 by Mughal emperor Shah Jahan, it is a stunning example of Mughal architecture. The mosque is made of red sandstone and marble and has three massive domes and two towering minarets. It can accommodate 25,000 people and is used for daily prayers by Muslims.

2. Taj-ul-Masjid, Bhopal: This mosque, located in Bhopal, Madhya Pradesh, is the largest mosque in India. It was built in the 19th century by Nawab Shah Jahan Begum, the queen of Bhopal. The mosque has an impressive architecture, with seven domes and four minarets, and is surrounded by a lush garden. The mosque is often used for religious ceremonies and is a popular tourist attraction.

3. Badshahi Mosque, Lahore: Built by Mughal emperor Aurangzeb in 1671, this mosque is one of the most beautiful mosques in India. It is made of red sandstone and marble and has four magnificent minarets and three domes. The mosque is used for daily prayers by Muslims and is a popular tourist attraction.

4. Moti Masjid, Agra: This stunning mosque, located in Agra, is one of the most popular mosques in India. It was built in 1648 by Mughal emperor Shah Jahan and is made of white marble. The mosque has three domes and four minarets and is often used for daily prayers by Muslims.

5. Charminar, Hyderabad: This iconic mosque, located in Hyderabad, is one of the most famous mosques in India. Built in 1591 by Sultan Muhammad Quli Qutb Shah, it is an impressive example of Islamic architecture. The mosque has four minarets and a large central dome and is used for daily prayers by Muslims.

6. Juma Masjid, Ahmedabad: Built in 1423 by Sultan Ahmed Shah, this impressive mosque is located in Ahmedabad. It has a grand architecture, with 15 domes and 260 pillars, and is used for daily prayers by Muslims. The mosque also has a large courtyard that is often used for cultural and religious activities.

7. Jami Masjid, Delhi: This majestic mosque, located in Delhi, was built in 1650 by Mughal emperor Shah Jahan. It is made of red sandstone and marble and has three domes and two minarets. The mosque is used for daily prayers by Muslims and is a popular tourist attraction.

8. Futtehpur Sikri, Agra: Built in 1571 by Mughal emperor Akbar, this majestic mosque is located in Agra. The mosque is made of red sandstone and marble and has three domes and two minarets. The mosque is used for daily prayers by Muslims and is a popular tourist attraction.

9. Aiwan-e-Begumpuri, Lucknow: This grand mosque, located in Lucknow, was built in the 18th century by Nawab Asaf-ud-Daula. The mosque has a grand architecture, with four imposing minarets and a large central dome. The mosque is used for daily prayers by Muslims and is a popular tourist attraction.

Chapter 4: Experiencing India.

India is one of the most culturally diverse countries in the world, and it's no wonder that travelers from around the globe flock to its many attractions. As a visitor to the country, there is truly no experience quite like experiencing India. From the stunning beauty of its landscapes to the unique aromas of its cuisine, India is a place of unparalleled appeal.

When visiting India, one of the first things you will notice is the vibrant culture. Everywhere you look, you will be surrounded by people of all walks of life, all of whom contribute to the dynamic and exciting atmosphere of the country. The diversity of the culture is reflected in the food, music, art, and architecture, all of which are integral parts of the Indian experience.

The hospitality and kindness of the people is another major attraction of India. Whether you're in a small village or a bustling city, you'll find that locals are eager to help out, even if they don't speak the same language as you. India is also known for its unique spiritual practices, which are both fascinating and inviting. From yoga and meditation to pilgrimages and temple visits, there is something for everyone when it comes to experiencing India's spiritual side.

The landscape of the country is also something that must be seen to be believed. From the magnificent

Himalayan Mountains to the lush green tea plantations of Kerala, India has something for everyone. Whether you're an avid hiker or a beach lover, India has something for you.

India is also a great destination for shopping. From colorful fabrics to exquisite jewelry, India has some of the most unique and beautiful items available. Whether you're looking for something exotic or something more traditional, you'll be sure to find it in India.

No matter what you're looking for, India has something to offer everyone. From stunning landscapes to vibrant culture and spiritual practices, India is a place that can be experienced in a multitude of ways. Whether you're a first-time visitor or a long-time resident, India is sure to make an impression that will last a lifetime.

Cultural Experiences

India is a country full of cultural experiences. From ancient customs and rituals to vibrant festivals, India offers a vast range of cultural experiences to explore.

India's culture is a unique blend of many ancient traditions and customs. Its culture is shaped by its rich history, diverse geography, and overwhelming population. Every region of India has its own distinct customs and traditions. From the vibrant street markets and colorful festivals to the ancient architecture and religious beliefs, India's culture is an endless source of fascination.

One of the best ways to experience India's culture is to explore the country's vibrant festivals. India celebrates a wide variety of festivals throughout the year, and each one has its own unique customs and traditions. From the Holi festival of colors to the Diwali festival of lights and the Ganesh Chaturthi festival of Lord Ganesha, there's something for everyone to enjoy.

India is also home to some of the world's most famous monuments and historical sites. From the Taj Mahal in Agra to the Red Fort in Delhi and the Ajanta and Ellora caves in Maharashtra, India's ancient monuments and architecture are sure to leave a lasting impression.

The food in India is another important part of the country's culture. Indian cuisine is a combination of many different regional specialties, and each region has its own unique flavors and ingredients. From the spicy curries of the south to the sweet desserts of the north, Indian food is sure to tantalize the taste buds.

Finally, India's vibrant art and music scene is an integral part of the country's culture. From the classical music of the north to the tribal music of the east, and from the traditional folk dances of the west to the modern art of the south, India's art and music is a true reflection of its diverse culture.

India is home to many wonderful cultural experiences, and its culture is sure to leave a lasting impression on all who visit. Whether you're exploring India's vibrant festivals, monuments, cuisine, or art and music, India's culture is sure to provide an unforgettable experience.

Adventure Activities

Adventure activities in India are gaining attention in recent years and people from all across the world are coming to the country to experience the thrill and excitement of these activities. India provides a wide range of adventure activities that include trekking, mountaineering, rock climbing, kayaking, rafting, paragliding, skiing, surfing, and much more. Here is a detailed list of the most popular adventure activities in India:

1. Trekking: Trekking is one of the most popular adventure activities in India as it provides a great opportunity to explore the beautiful landscapes and rugged terrain of the Himalayas. Trekkers can experience the thrill of crossing high passes, sleeping in tents, and camping in the wilderness. Some of the popular trekking destinations in India include Kashmir, Ladakh, Sikkim, Himachal Pradesh, and Uttarakhand.

2. Mountaineering: Mountaineering is another popular adventure activity in India, and it involves scaling some of the highest peaks of the Himalayas. It is a perfect way to challenge yourself and explore the unknown. Some of the popular mountaineering destinations in India include Ladakh, Sikkim, Uttarakhand, Himachal Pradesh, and Kashmir.

3. Rock Climbing: Rock Climbing is a great way to test your physical strength and skills, and it is one of the most popular adventure activities in India. It is a great way to explore the rugged terrain of the Himalayas and challenge yourself to conquer the highest peaks. Some of the popular destinations for rock climbing in India include Uttarakhand, Himachal Pradesh, Kashmir, and Ladakh.

4. Kayaking: Kayaking is another popular adventure activity in India and it involves paddling a kayak through the waters of rivers and lakes. It is a great way to explore the serene and tranquil waters of the country and experience the thrill of white water rafting. Some of the popular destinations for kayaking in India include the Ganges, Brahmaputra, Cauvery, and Narmada Rivers.

5. Rafting: Rafting is one of the most thrilling adventure activities in India and it involves navigating the turbulent waters of rivers and streams. It is a great way to explore the country's wilderness and experience the thrills of tackling the rapids. Some of the popular destinations for rafting in India include the Ganges, Brahmaputra, Cauvery, and Narmada Rivers.

6. Paragliding: Paragliding is a great way to experience the thrill of soaring high in the sky and it is one of the most popular adventure activities in India. It is a great way to explore the scenic beauty of the Himalayas and challenge yourself to take off from the highest peak. Some of the popular destinations for paragliding in India include Dharamsala, Manali, and Bir Billing.

7. Skiing: Skiing is another popular adventure activity in India and it involves skiing on the snow-covered slopes of the Himalayas. It is a great way to beat the winter chills and experience the thrill of skiing in the snow. Some of the popular skiing destinations in India include Manali, Gulmarg, and Auli.

8. Surfing: Surfing is one of the most popular adventure activities in India and it involves riding the waves of the Arabian Sea. It is a great way to explore the pristine beaches of the country and experience the thrill of riding the waves of the ocean. Some of the popular surfing destinations in India include Goa, Kovalam, and Gokarna.

India is a paradise for adventure enthusiasts and it offers a wide range of activities that cater to different skill levels and interests. Whether you are looking for a thrilling adventure activity or a peaceful experience, India has something for everyone. So, get ready to experience the thrill of these adventure activities in India and make your vacation even more memorable.

Nature and Wildlife

India is a country of diverse landscapes, ranging from the snow-capped Himalayas in the north to the tropical jungles of the south. India is blessed with a rich variety of wildlife, ranging from majestic tigers and elephants to the colorful peacock, and abundant birdlife. India is home to over 500 species of mammals, 1,200 species of birds, and more than 2,000 species of reptiles.

India is home to some of the most spectacular wildlife habitats in the world and is a popular destination for wildlife lovers. The country has 89 national parks and 515 wildlife sanctuaries, which are havens for a great variety of wildlife. Some of the most popular wildlife sanctuaries in India include Jim Corbett National Park, Ranthambore National Park, and Kaziranga National Park. These parks and sanctuaries are home to an incredible variety of wildlife, including tigers, elephants, rhinos, leopards, deer, and many other species.

India is also home to some of the most vibrant and diverse flora and fauna in the world. The country is home to a vast array of plants, including mangroves, tropical rainforests, and grasslands. India is also home to a wide range of animals, including monkeys, bears, snakes, and many more.

India has a long and rich history of protecting its wildlife. The Indian Wildlife Protection Act of 1972 provides legal protection of the country's wildlife, and the government has taken a number of initiatives to conserve the country's biodiversity. The government has also established a number of conservation programs and sanctuaries, which help to protect India's wildlife.

India is a fantastic destination for those who are looking to experience the beauty and diversity of its wildlife. Whether you are looking to view majestic tigers in the forests of Jim Corbett National Park or explore the jungles of Ranthambore, India is sure to provide you with an unforgettable wildlife experience.

India is also home to a range of fascinating aquatic creatures, including dolphins, whales, and turtles. The country has 26 Ramsar Sites, which are wetlands of international importance, and these are home to a number of aquatic animals. India also has some of the most diverse and vibrant marine life in the world, with a variety of coral reefs and mangrove forests.

The Indian government has taken a number of steps to protect its wildlife, including the establishment of a number of reserves and sanctuaries. These reserves and sanctuaries are vital for the conservation of India's rare and endangered species, and provide an important refuge for wildlife.

India is also home to a range of unique and fascinating cultures, and many of these cultures have a deep connection to the natural world and its wildlife. India has a long tradition of wildlife conservation and has a number of traditional conservation practices. The government is also working to promote wildlife tourism, which is becoming increasingly popular in India.

India is a stunning country with a wealth of wildlife, and it is a great destination for those who are looking to experience nature and its wildlife in all its glory. Whether you are looking to explore the jungles of the south, take in the majestic views of the Himalayas, or observe the abundant wildlife in India's national parks and sanctuaries, India is sure to offer you an unforgettable wildlife experience.

Traditional Dishes

India is a land of spices and flavourful cuisine, with dishes that vary from region to region. Traditional Indian dishes are as diverse and intricate as the country's culture and history, and feature an abundance of ingredients and cooking techniques. From spicy curries to sweet desserts, here is a list of some of the most popular traditional dishes in India.

1. Chicken Tikka Masala: This dish is a staple of Indian cuisine, and is made with pieces of boneless chicken marinated in yogurt, spices and herbs, then cooked in a creamy tomato-based sauce.

2. Butter Chicken: This creamy and rich dish is a classic in North Indian cuisine. The chicken is marinated in a blend of spices and yogurt before being cooked in a tomato-butter based sauce.

3. Dal Makhani: This popular lentil dish is made with black gram and red kidney beans, cooked in a creamy tomato-based sauce and flavoured with spices.

4. Biryani: This delicious dish is made with a blend of spices, rice, and either chicken, beef, lamb, or fish. The rice is cooked in a mixture of spices, herbs, and yoghurt.

5. Samosas: These deep-fried pastries are filled with a variety of fillings, including potatoes, peas, onions, and spices.

6. Aloo Gobi: This popular North Indian dish is made with potatoes and cauliflower, cooked in a blend of spices and herbs.

7. Paneer Butter Masala: This dish is made with cubes of paneer (Indian cottage cheese) cooked in a creamy tomato-based sauce.

8. Chana Masala: Chana masala is a popular vegetarian dish made with chickpeas cooked in a blend of spices and onions.

9. Paratha: Parathas are flatbreads made with a variety of flours, including wheat, gram, and corn. They can be stuffed with a variety of fillings, including potatoes, paneer, and spices.

10. Gulab Jamun: Gulab jamun is a popular Indian dessert made with deep-fried milk balls soaked in a sugary syrup.

11. Kofta: Kofta is a dish made with ground meat or vegetables that have been mixed with spices and herbs and then fried or steamed.

12. Achari Paneer: Achari paneer is a dish made with paneer (Indian cottage cheese), cooked in pickling spices, onions, tomatoes, and a variety of herbs.

13. Palak Paneer: Palak paneer is a dish made with cubes of paneer (Indian cottage cheese) cooked in a creamy spinach-based sauce.

14. Bhindi Masala: Bhindi masala is a dish made with okra, onions, and a variety of spices.

15. Vada Pav: Vada Pav is a popular snack in Maharashtra, made with a spicy potato mixture that is deep-fried and served in a bun.

16. Idli Sambar: Idli sambar is a popular South Indian dish made with steamed rice cakes served with a lentil-based sauce.

17. Pani Puri: Pani puri is a popular street food throughout India, made with crisp fried dough balls filled with a variety of fillings, such as potatoes, onions, and spices, and served with a spicy mint-coriander sauce.

18. Naan: Naan is a type of flatbread made with a variety of flours, including wheat and gram. It is cooked in a tandoor oven and served with a variety of curries or dips.

19. Kheer: Kheer is a popular Indian dessert made with milk, rice, and sugar and flavoured with cardamom, saffron, and other spices.

20. Dosa: Dosa is a type of pancake made with a fermented batter of rice and lentils. It is usually served with a variety of accompaniments, such as chutney or sambar.

India is a land of diverse and intricate cuisine, and these are just some of the traditional dishes that make up this unique and flavourful cuisine. From curries to desserts, the traditional dishes in India are sure to tantalize your taste buds.

Local Wines

India has a long and varied history of winemaking, and the local wines of India are some of the best in the world. With a diverse range of grape varieties, flavors, and styles, Indian wines are becoming increasingly popular in the international market. Here is a list of some of the best local wines in India that you should try.

1. Sula Vineyards: Sula is one of the most popular wineries in India and their wines are some of the best quality. They offer a range of red, white, and sparkling wines, with some of the more popular varieties being Zinfandel, Chenin Blanc, and Sauvignon Blanc.

2. Grover Zampa Vineyards: This winery is known for producing premium quality wines, with some of the finest reds coming from their vineyards. Their most popular varieties are Cabernet Sauvignon, Shiraz, and Viognier.

3. Château Indage: This winery is known for producing some of the best sparkling wines in India, with their signature Brut being particularly popular. They also offer a range of still wines, including Cabernet Sauvignon and Sauvignon Blanc.

4. Four Seasons Vineyards: This winery is known for their award-winning reds, with their Cabernet Sauvignon and Shiraz being particularly popular. They also offer a range of whites and sparkling wines.

5. Fratelli Wines: This winery is known for producing some of the best quality sparkling wines in India, with their Brut and Brut Rosé being particularly popular. They also offer a range of still wines, including Cabernet Sauvignon, Chardonnay, and Sauvignon Blanc.

6. York Winery: This winery is known for producing some of the best quality red wines in India, with their Cabernet Sauvignon and Merlot being particularly popular. They also offer a range of whites, sparkling wines, and fortified wines.

7. Nine Hills Winery: This winery is known for producing some of the best quality white wines in India, with their Chenin Blanc and Sauvignon Blanc being particularly popular. They also offer a range of reds, sparkling wines, and fortified wines.

8. Grover Art Collection: This winery is known for producing some of the finest reds in India, with their Cabernet Sauvignon and Shiraz being particularly popular. They also offer a range of whites and sparkling wines.

9. Four Seasons Winery: This winery is known for producing some of the best quality sparkling wines in India, with their Brut and Brut Rosé being particularly popular. They also offer a range of still wines, including Cabernet Sauvignon, Chardonnay, and Sauvignon Blanc.

10. Indage Vintners: This winery is known for producing some of the finest reds in India, with their Cabernet Sauvignon and Shiraz being particularly popular. They also offer a range of whites and sparkling wines.

India has come a long way in the world of winemaking, and the local wines of India are some of the best in the world. With so many different varieties and styles to choose from, it is easy to find something that you will enjoy. So why not try one of these local wines today? Cheers!

Rustic Food and Drinks

India is home to some of the world's most succulent and luscious rustic food and drinks. From a variety of curries to road food, India has a commodity for everyone. The rustic food and drinks of India offer a unique flavor profile that is sure to tantalize the taste kiddies. also's a list of some of the most popular rustic food and drinks in India:

Curries:

Indian curries are famed for their bold, luscious taste. Popular curries include the classic funk tikka masala, paneer adulation masala, dal makhani, kadai paneer, and multitudinous further.

Chaat:

Chaat is a type of Indian road food that is generally made with potatoes, spices, and chutneys. Popular chaat dishes include pani puri, bhel puri, dahi puri, and aloo tikki chaat.

Paratha:

Parathas are a type of Indian flatbread that are generally served with curries, chutneys, and pickles. Popular parathas include aloo paratha, paneer paratha, and mooli paratha.

Samosa:

Samosas are a popular Indian snack made with a savory filling of potatoes, peas, and spices. They are generally served with chutneys and gravies.

Tandoori:

Tandoori dishes are generally cooked in a complexion rotisserie and are marinated with spices and yogurt before cookery. Popular tandoori dishes include tandoori funk, tandoori fish, and tandoori paneer.

Kebabs:

Kebabs are a type of grilled meat that is generally marinated in spices and yogurt before cookery. Popular kebabs include funk tikka, shami kebab, and seekh kebab.

Lassi:

Lassi is a popular yogurt- predicated drink that is generally seasoned with spices, nuts, or fruits. It's generally served as a stimulating drink or as a side dish to a mess.

Chai:

Chai is a popular Indian tea that is generally made with a mix of spices, milk, and sugar. It's constantly served with snacks or as a stimulating drink.

Rasmalai:

Rasmalai is a popular delicacy that is generally made with milk, cream, sugar, and saffron. It's generally served astounded and excelled with nuts, raisins, and cardamom. These are just a numerous of the succulent rustic food and drinks that India has to offer. Whether you 're looking for a quick snack or a full mess, India has a commodity for everyone. So, the coming time you 're in India, be sure to try some of these rustic dishes and drinks. No matter where you travel in India, you can find an array of rustic food and drinks that offer unique flavors and aromas. From curries to road food, Indian cuisine is full of flavor and is sure to please indeed the pickiest of eaters. Whether you 're looking for a light snack or a full mess, India has a commodity for everyone. In addition to its succulent curries, India is also home to a variety of chaat dishes, parathas, samosas, and kebabs. Chaat is a type of Indian road food that is generally made with potatoes, spices, and chutneys. Parathas are a type of Indian flatbread that are generally served with curries, chutneys, and pickles. Samosas are a popular Indian snack made with a savory filling of potatoes, peas, and spices. Kebabs are a type of grilled meat that is generally marinated in spices and yogurt before cooking. India is also home to a variety of drinks that are sure to tantalize the taste kiddies. Popular drinks include lassi, a yogurt- predicated drink that is generally seasoned with spices, nuts, or fruits, and chai, a popular Indian tea that is generally made with a mix of spices, milk, and sugar. For a sweet treat, try rasmalai, a popular delicacy that is generally made with milk, cream, sugar, and saffron. When it comes to rustic food and drinks, India has a commodity for everyone. From a variety of curries to road food, Indian cuisine is full of flavor and is sure to please indeed the pickiest of eaters. So, the coming time you 're in India, be sure to try some of these rustic dishes and drinks.

Craft Beer

Craft beer in India is one of the fastest-growing segments of the beer market. It is a type of beer that is brewed in small batches, often with local ingredients, and is typically made with a unique flavor and aroma. Craft beer is often considered to be a specialty beer, as it is often made with a variety of different ingredients and flavors that give it a unique taste and aroma.

Craft beer has been gaining popularity in India in recent years, with a number of craft breweries opening up across the country. These breweries are often small, independent operations, and specialize in producing handcrafted, small-batch beers with unique, local ingredients. Many of these craft beers have a distinct flavor, aroma, and body that sets them apart from the regular beer brands.

The craft beer scene in India has been growing rapidly in recent years, with a number of craft beer festivals, competitions, and other events being held for craft beer lovers. Craft beer is becoming increasingly popular in the country, and is often seen as a way to explore the local culture and flavors of the country.

Some of the most popular craft beers in India include White Owl, Bira 91, Simba, and The White Owl. These craft beers are often made with a variety of different ingredients and flavors, such as wheat, barley, hops, and spices, and are often made with local ingredients. These craft beers are often served on tap at pubs and bars, or in bottles and cans at liquor stores.

Craft beer in India is becoming increasingly popular, and is a great way to explore the local culture and flavors of the country. With the increasing number of craft breweries opening up in the country, craft beer is becoming more accessible and popular, and is a great way to experience the unique flavors of India.

Chapter 5: Practical Information.

India is a country with a vibrant artistic history and a wealth of activities to engage visitors. India is a vastly diverse nation, ranging from the frenetic activity of its megalopolises to the tranquil serenity of its countryside. India offers a memorable experience to those who travel there thanks to its rich culture, hospitable people, and diverse choreographies. A complete list of useful facts about India is also provided to help you make the most of your stay.

1. VISAS All visitors to India must have a current visa. Through the Indian High Commission or Consulate in your nation, visas can be obtained. Please be aware that applying for a visa could take several weeks.

2. CURRENCY. The Indian Rupee (INR) is the country's legal tender. The Indian Rupee's currency rate changes every day. Credit cards are accepted at many businesses, and ATMs are widely available.

3. GETTING AROUND India has a vast network of air routes, roadways, and roads. The most convenient mode of transportation within India is via air, but there are also railways and automobiles.

4. CLIMATE There are several climates in India, from tropical in the south to moderate in the north. Most of the country can see showers that last up to four months. India is typically a safe place to travel to, but visitors should always use caution and abide by local regulations.

5. HEALTH Drinking tap water is unsafe, and visitors should take precautions to avoid contracting illnesses that are spread through food. For travel to India, travelers are advised to get the necessary shots, and they should also purchase comprehensive travel insurance.

6. COMMUNICATION English is widely spoken in India, and the majority of people in large megalopolises are able to grasp basic English.

7. FOOD Indian cuisine is diverse, ranging from the sassy curries of the north to the seafood in the south. Most cafes provide accommodating options, and many also provide halal food.

8. SHOPPING India is a terrific place to go shopping because there are so many items at great costs. Logrolling should be done with respect as it is expected.

9. CULTURE India is a diverse country in terms of communities and ideologies. Visitors must be careful to uphold native customs and traditions and should dress modestly. There is something for everyone in the unfathomable country of India. With the correct medication, you can get the most out of your trip and have a memorable one

.

Accommodations

Accommodation in India ranges from five-star luxury hotels to budget-friendly properties and everything in between. Whether you're looking for a beachside resort or a heritage hotel, India has something to offer. Here is a comprehensive list of accommodations in India.

1. Hotels: India has some of the finest luxury hotels in the world. Many of these hotels offer world-class amenities such as swimming pools, spas, and fitness centers. Popular hotel chains in India include Taj Hotels, Oberoi Hotels, Leela Palace, ITC Hotels, and Marriott Hotels.

2. Resorts: India is home to some of the most luxurious resorts in the world. From beach resorts to hillside retreats, India has something to offer for every kind of traveler. Popular resort chains in India include Anantara, Taj Exotica, Oberoi Resorts, and ITC Grand Resorts.

3. Guest Houses: If you're looking for a more intimate experience, then a guest house might be a better option for you. They are usually less expensive than hotels and offer a more homely atmosphere. Popular guest houses in India include the Taj Guest House, ITC Maratha, Gokarna Beach Cottages, and Neemrana Fort Palace.

4. Homestays: Homestays are a great way to experience Indian culture and hospitality. They are usually owned and operated by local families and offer a more personal experience than a hotel. Popular homestays in India include the Ela Eco Lodges, Meghalaya Homestays, and the Kumaon Homestays.

5. Hostels: Hostels are another great budget-friendly option for accommodation in India. They offer basic amenities such as beds, showers, and Wi-Fi. Popular hostels in India include the Zostel, GoStops, and the Hostelling International India.

Whether you're looking for a luxurious stay or a budget-friendly accommodation, India has something to offer for every kind of traveler. With its diverse range of accommodations, India is a great destination for any kind of traveler.

Hotel

India is an amazing country with an array of accommodation options, from luxurious 5-star hotels to budget-friendly hostels. Whether you're looking for a romantic getaway or a family vacation, there's a hotel in India to suit every budget and taste.

Here is a list of some of the best hotels in India:

1. The Oberoi Udaivilas, Udaipur

The Oberoi Udaivilas is the perfect place to stay if you're looking for a luxurious and romantic experience. Located on the banks of Lake Pichola in Udaipur, this 5-star hotel offers breathtaking views of the lake and the surrounding Aravalli Hills. The hotel is renowned for its warm hospitality and excellent service. It features an outdoor swimming pool, spa, and fitness centre, as well as several delicious restaurants.

2. The Taj Mahal Palace, Mumbai

The Taj Mahal Palace is one of India's most iconic hotels. Located in the heart of Mumbai, this luxurious 5-star hotel offers spectacular views of the Arabian Sea and the Gateway of India. The hotel features an array of restaurants, a spa, and a fitness centre, as well as a host of recreational activities.

3. The Lalit, New Delhi

The Lalit is a 5-star hotel located in the heart of New Delhi. This hotel is renowned for its modern design and luxurious amenities, including an outdoor swimming pool, spa, and fitness centre. The hotel also offers a range of dining options, from fine dining restaurants to casual cafes.

4. Vivanta by Taj, Goa

Vivanta by Taj is located in the stunning beach destination of Goa. This 5-star hotel offers spectacular views of the Arabian Sea and the surrounding palm trees. The hotel features an array of luxurious amenities, including an outdoor swimming pool, spa, and fitness centre. It also offers a variety of dining options and recreational activities.

5. The Leela Palace, Chennai

The Leela Palace is a luxurious 5-star hotel located in the heart of Chennai. This hotel offers stunning views of the Bay of Bengal, as well as a host of luxurious amenities, such as an outdoor swimming pool, spa, and fitness centre. The hotel also offers a range of delicious restaurants and recreational activities.

6. The Park, Kolkata

The Park is a 5-star hotel located in the heart of Kolkata. This hotel offers breathtaking views of the Hooghly River and the surrounding cityscape. The hotel features an array of luxurious amenities, including an outdoor swimming pool, spa, and fitness centre. It also offers a range of delicious restaurants and recreational activities.

7. The Leela Ambience, Gurugram

The Leela Ambience is a 5-star hotel located in the heart of Gurugram. This hotel offers spectacular views of the Aravalli Hills and the surrounding cityscape. The hotel features an array of luxurious amenities, such as an outdoor swimming pool, spa, and fitness center. It also offers a range of delicious restaurants and recreational activities.

8. The LaLiT Ashok Bangalore

The LaLiT Ashok Bangalore is a 5-star hotel located in the heart of the city. This hotel offers stunning views of the cityscape and the surrounding lakes. The hotel features an array of luxurious amenities, including an outdoor swimming pool, spa, and fitness center. It also offers a range of delicious restaurants and recreational activities.

No matter where you're headed, there's a hotel in India to suit every budget and taste. From luxurious 5-star hotels to budget-friendly hostels, India has something to offer for everyone.

Hostels

India is an incredibly diverse country with a rich cultural heritage, stunning landscapes, and delicious cuisine. It is also home to a vast array of accommodation options, ranging from luxury resorts to budget friendly hostels. Hostels in India offer a unique experience, allowing travelers to stay in a communal environment, meet fellow travelers, and enjoy the local culture.

Hostels provide a great way to explore India on a budget, as they are significantly cheaper than hotels or resorts. They can also be a great option for solo travelers, as they often provide the opportunity to meet like-minded people.

Below is a list of the best hostels in India, all of which offer great amenities and a unique experience:

1. Zostel, Delhi: Zostel is a chain of hostels located in major cities across India. The Delhi branch is located in the heart of the city and offers a range of facilities such as free WiFi, air-conditioned rooms, and a rooftop terrace.

2. Backpacker Panda, Mumbai: This hostel is located in the trendy Bandra West neighborhood of Mumbai. It has a great selection of rooms and facilities, including a lounge area, a terrace, and a café.

3. Madpackers Hostel, Pune: This hostel is located in the vibrant Koregaon Park area of Pune. It offers a variety of rooms and facilities, including a rooftop garden, a café, and a common lounge area.

4. The Hosteller, Bangalore: The Hosteller is a modern hostel located in the heart of Bangalore. It offers a selection of rooms, a café, a terrace, and a common lounge area.

5. The Yellow Hostel, Goa: This hostel is located in the popular Anjuna Beach area of Goa. It offers a variety of rooms and facilities, including a lounge area, a café, and a bar.

6. Hostel 9, Chennai: Hostel 9 is located in the lively Mylapore area of Chennai. It offers a range of rooms and facilities, including a rooftop terrace, a café, and a common lounge area.

7. The Backpacker Co., Hyderabad: This hostel is located in the lively Banjara Hills area of Hyderabad. It offers a selection of rooms and facilities, including a rooftop terrace, a café, and a common lounge area.

These hostels provide a great way to explore India on a budget and are sure to give you a unique and memorable experience. Whether you're a solo traveler or a group of friends, these hostels will provide you with comfortable and affordable accommodation. So, go ahead and book your stay at one of these amazing hostels in India!

Camping

Camping in India is a popular outdoor activity for travelers looking to enjoy the natural beauty of the country. With its vast network of rivers, forests, mountains, deserts, and beaches, India offers a wide variety of camping experiences for adventure seekers and nature lovers alike. Whether you're looking to stay in luxurious tented camps, rustic jungle lodges, or even on a houseboat, there are plenty of camping opportunities to choose from in India.

Tented Camps: Tented camps are one of the most popular camping options in India. Many of these camps are located in scenic locations with easy access to nearby attractions, such as national parks, wildlife sanctuaries, and historical sites. The tents come in different sizes, ranging from basic to luxurious. Most of these camps offer amenities such as running water, electricity, hot showers, and even air conditioning.

Jungle Lodges: For those looking for a more rustic camping experience, jungle lodges are the perfect option. These lodges usually have basic amenities and are located in remote areas of the jungles. Adventure seekers will enjoy exploring the lush vegetation and spotting wildlife from the comfort of their lodges.

Houseboats: Houseboats are a great way to experience camping in India. These boats are usually equipped with basic amenities and provide travelers with the opportunity to explore rivers and lakes in a unique and exciting way.

Beach Camps: For those looking to relax and soak up the sun, beach camps are the ideal option.

These camps are located on the serene beaches of India and provide travelers with the opportunity to enjoy the views of the ocean and the sound of the waves.

Camping in India is a great way to explore the country and experience its natural beauty. Whether you're looking for a luxurious tented camp, a rustic jungle lodge, or even a houseboat, there are plenty of camping options available for travelers of all interests. So, grab your tent and hit the road for an unforgettable camping trip to India.

Transportation

In India, transportation plays a significant role in both the infrastructure and economics of the nation. The nation requires an advanced transportation system to carry people and products effectively given its population of nearly 1.2 billion. India has one of the greatest transportation systems in the world, which includes highways, railroads, airports, ports, and waterways.

Roads: With a network of more than 4.6 million kilometers, India is home to the second-largest road system in the world. National Highways, Expressways, State Highways, and other highways make up its divisions. The National Highways, which connect major cities and towns all across the nation and have a length of more than 68,000 km, are the most significant. They are often toll highways that are maintained by India's National Highways Authority.

Railway: The largest and most established railroad system in Asia is the Indian Railways. It connects practically all of the major cities and towns in the nation and has a total length of about 65,000 km. With more than 1.5 million workers on its payroll, it is one of the biggest employers in the world. A significant source of transportation for both freight and passengers, the Indian Railways is one of the most effective rail networks in the world.

Airports: India is home to more than 350 airports, making it one of the world's largest aviation networks. The Airports Authority of India (AAI) is in charge of managing and owning airports. India has several important airports, including Indira Gandhi International Airport in Delhi, Chhatrapati Shivaji International Airport in Mumbai, and Netaji Subhash Chandra Bose International Airport in Kolkata.

Ports: India has more than 200 minor ports in addition to 14 large ports along its more than 6,000 kilometers of coastline. Major ports include those in Paradip, Mumbai, Kandla, Cochin, and Visakhapatnam. In addition to this, the nation also possesses a number of interior rivers that are utilized for the transportation of both products and people.

Public Transport: Buses and railroads make up the majority of India's public transportation system. While railways are the primary means of transportation for long distance travel, bus services are provided in the majority of cities. With over 22 million passengers per day, the Indian Railways is the world's largest passenger airline. Auto-rickshaws, taxis, and cycle-rickshaws are some more forms of public transportation in India.

India has a well-developed transportation system overall, which is continually upgraded to meet the demands of its sizable population. To increase the effectiveness and dependability of its transportation services and infrastructure, the government is making significant investments.

India is investing in new technology like driverless automobiles, high-speed rail networks, and electric vehicles in addition to the conventional modes of transportation. It is anticipated that these technologies would transform travel by making it cheaper and faster. Additionally, the government is making efforts to make the roadways safer and less congested. This entails putting in place stronger regulations for automobile emissions, implementing high-occupancy vehicle lanes, and utilizing cutting-edge traffic management technology.

The government is also implementing affordable public transportation options including metro and bus rapid transit systems to ensure that all individuals, regardless of their socioeconomic standing, have access to transportation. Traveling will be simpler as a result, especially in urban areas where traffic congestion is a major issue.

Overall, India is rapidly changing its transportation system to meet the country's expanding demand. India's transportation system is set to keep getting better in the years to come thanks to the government's significant investments in safety, technology, and infrastructure.

Visas and Documentation

Visas and Documentation in India

India is a country with a rich and diverse culture, making it a popular destination for tourists and expats. Therefore, it is important to understand the process of obtaining visas and documentation in order to travel to India. The Indian government has instituted various types of visas and documentation that are required for various purposes.

Tourist Visas

The most common type of visa for travelers to India is a Tourist visa. This type of visa allows travelers to stay in India for up to six months. Applications for tourist visas can be made online or through the Indian Embassy in the applicant's country of residence. Applicants will need to provide proof of their travel plans, as well as proof of financial means to support their stay.

Business Visas

Business visas are issued to travelers who plan to conduct business activities in India. This type of visa is valid for up to five years, and applicants must demonstrate proof of their business plans in India. Business visas can be obtained through the Indian Embassy in the applicant's country of residence.

Student Visas

Foreign students who plan to study in India must obtain a Student visa. Student visas are valid for up to five years and applicants will need to provide proof of their admission to an Indian university or institute. Student visa applications can be made online or through the Indian Embassy in the applicant's country of residence.

Employment Visas

Employment visas are issued to foreign workers who plan to work in India. This type of visa is valid for up to three years, and applicants must provide proof of their employment offer in India. Employment visa applications can be made online or through the Indian Embassy in the applicant's country of residence.

Medical Visas

Medical visas are issued to travelers who plan to receive medical treatment in India. This type of visa is valid for up to one year, and applicants must provide proof of their medical condition in order to obtain the visa. Medical visas can be obtained through the Indian Embassy in the applicant's country of residence.

In conclusion, it is important to understand the process of obtaining visas and documentation for travel to India. Tourists, business travelers, students, and workers must all obtain the appropriate visa for their purpose, and provide the necessary documentation for their stay in India. India. Tourists, business travelers, students, and workers must all obtain the appropriate visa for their purpose, and provide the necessary documentation for their stay in India

.

Money and Banking

Money and banking in India is an important part of the country's economic system. It is responsible for providing the necessary funds to support economic growth and development. Money and banking in India is regulated by the Reserve Bank of India (RBI) which is responsible for formulating and implementing monetary policy.

The Indian banking system consists of the Scheduled Commercial Banks (SCBs) and Non-Scheduled Banks (NSBs). SCBs are further classified into three categories – Public Sector Banks (PSBs), Private Sector Banks (PVBs) and Foreign Banks (FBs).

Public Sector Banks are owned and managed by the Government of India and include State Bank of India (SBI), Punjab National Bank (PNB), Bank of

Baroda (BoB) and Canara Bank. Private Sector Banks include ICICI Bank, HDFC Bank, Axis Bank and Kotak Mahindra Bank. Foreign Banks are those which are registered in foreign countries, but have branches in India.

The banking system in India is regulated by various laws, such as the Banking Regulation Act, 1949, the Deposit Insurance and Credit Guarantee Corporation Act, 1961, the Negotiable Instruments Act, 1881 and the Banking Ombudsman Scheme, 2006. These laws have been enacted to ensure the safety and security of banking transactions and to protect the interests of customers.

The Reserve Bank of India is also responsible for regulating the currency and monetary policy of India. It is responsible for issuing currency notes and coins, managing foreign exchange reserves and regulating the flow of credit in the economy. The RBI also sets the repo rate and reverse repo rate, which are used to influence the cost of credit in the economy.

Another important function of the banking system in India is to provide banking services such as savings and current accounts, fixed deposits, debit and credit cards, money transfers and loans. Banks also provide a range of investment services such as mutual funds, stocks and bonds.

In India, banks are also responsible for issuing and managing digital payments such as Unified Payment Interface (UPI). UPI is a digital payment system which allows customers to transfer funds from one bank account to another using their mobile phone.

In addition, the banking system in India is used by the government for implementing various social and economic welfare programmes. These programmes include the Mahatma Gandhi National Rural Employment Guarantee Act (MGNREGA), Pradhan Mantri Awas Yojana (PMAY), Pradhan Mantri Fasal Bima Yojana (PMFBY) and Ujjwala Yojana. Banks are also providing banking services to farmers and small businesses under different government schemes such as the Pradhan Mantri Mudra Yojana (PMMY). The banking system in India is also responsible for providing credit to businesses and individuals. Banks offer different types of loans such as home loans, car loans, business loans and personal loans. Banks provide these loans to individuals and businesses at an interest rate determined by the Reserve Bank of India.

Overall, the banking system in India plays a key role in the country's economy. It provides banking services, ensures financial inclusion, implements government schemes and provides credit to businesses and individuals. It is an important part of the Indian economy and plays a crucial role in the country's development.

Chapter 6: Great Itineraries.

India is an amazing country with a plethora of stunning locations to explore. From the towering Himalayas in the North to the stunning beaches of Goa in the South, India has something to offer for travelers of all types. Whether you're looking for a romantic getaway, an adventure filled holiday, or a cultural tour, there's a great itinerary for you to explore in India. Here are some of the best itineraries to check out in India:

1. Golden Triangle Tour: This classic itinerary takes you to the cultural capitals of India - Delhi, Agra and Jaipur. Start your journey in Delhi and explore its famous monuments like the Red Fort and Qutub Minar. Then, head to Agra and witness the beauty of the Taj Mahal. Finally, end your trip in Jaipur and marvel at the magnificent palaces and forts of the Pink City.

2. Beaches of Goa: If you're looking for a paradise beach holiday, then head to Goa. With its stunning beaches, vibrant nightlife, shacks and cafes, Goa is the perfect destination for a fun-filled getaway. Don't miss out on exploring the famous churches as well.

3. Himalayan Trek: For the adventurous traveler, the Himalayas offer a spectacular trekking experience. From easy treks to challenging ones, there is something for everyone here. So, pack your bags and embark on a journey of exploration and adventure.

4. Wildlife Safari: India is home to a variety of wildlife. From tigers and leopards in the national parks to wild elephants in the jungles, a wildlife safari is a must-do in India.

5. Ayurveda Tour: India is also known for its ancient medicinal practices. An Ayurveda tour will take you to some of the most famous Ayurveda centers in India where you can relax and rejuvenate.

6. Spiritual Tour: India is filled with spiritual sites and destinations. Take a spiritual tour and explore the many holy sites like Varanasi, Tirupati, Rishikesh and many more.

7. Hill Stations Tour: India is home to some of the most beautiful hill stations like Shimla, Nainital and Darjeeling. Take a tour of these stunning locations and soak in the beauty of nature.

So, if you're looking for a great itinerary in India, then these are some of the best options to explore. So, what are you waiting for? Pack your bags and head out to explore the beautiful country of India.

Two Weeks in India

India is a vibrant and diverse country that offers travellers a multitude of experiences. From the hill stations of the Himalayas to the beaches of Goa, India has something for everyone. Whether you're looking to relax and take in the sights or explore the culture, there's a perfect two-week itinerary waiting for you. Here is a suggested two-week itinerary for India that will help you make the most of your time in this amazing country.

Day 1: Arrive in Delhi

Start your two weeks in India by arriving in the bustling capital of Delhi. Spend your first day exploring the iconic sights of New Delhi such as the Red Fort, Qutub Minar and Humayun's Tomb. Take a rickshaw ride through the bustling markets and don't forget to sample the delicious local cuisine.

Day 2: Taj Mahal, Agra

On day two, take a train to the beautiful city of Agra to visit the iconic Taj Mahal. This magnificent structure is one of the most breathtaking sites in the world and is the symbol of eternal love between Emperor Shah Jahan and his beloved wife. After exploring the Taj Mahal, take a tour of Agra Fort before returning to Delhi.

Day 3: Jaipur

On day three, embark on a road trip to the historical city of Jaipur, the Pink City. Explore the many markets and monuments like the City Palace and Hawa Mahal. After a busy day of sightseeing, take a ride up to the hilltop fort of Amber for stunning views of the city.

Day 4-5: Udaipur

Spend the next two days in the romantic city of Udaipur. Make sure to visit the stunning City Palace and take a boat ride on Lake Pichola. Enjoy the stunning sunsets and take a stroll around the tranquil lakefront.

Day 6-7: Ranthambore National Park

Take a day trip to the Ranthambore National Park to explore the wildlife and beautiful scenery. Take a jeep safari to spot tigers and other wildlife, and don't forget to take a boat ride on the lake.

Day 8-9: Varanasi

Spend two days in the spiritual city of Varanasi. Take a boat ride on the sacred Ganges and explore the many temples and ghats. Visit the famous Kashi Vishwanath Temple and take a stroll along the ghats.

Day 10-11: Goa

Take a flight to the beach paradise of Goa and spend two days exploring the many beaches and lush greenery. Enjoy the nightlife, visit the old

Portuguese churches and take a boat ride to explore the backwaters.

Day 12-13: Mumbai
Spend the last two days of your two weeks in India in the vibrant city of Mumbai. Explore the colonial architecture, visit the many markets and don't forget to take a stroll along the famous Marine Drive.

Day 14: Departure
On day 14, it's time to say goodbye to India and begin your journey home. Make sure to take with you the beautiful memories of your two weeks in India.

One Month in India

One Month in India
The varied landscapes, civilizations, and climates of India make it an intriguing place to travel to and explore. Only a few of the many attractions India has to offer the adventurous traveler include the majestic Himalayas in the north and the tranquil backwaters of Kerala in the south. Below is a list of everything you might encounter during your first month in India.

On days 1-4, take a trip to Delhi and start exploring. Take a stroll through the city's lively streets, stunning landmarks, and hopping markets. For more information on the city and its past, take a rickshaw tour.

On days 5-7, visitors to Agra can visit the Taj Mahal by taking a train. Take a stroll through the neighborhood as you admire the magnificence of this magnificent landmark.

Visit Jaipur, the Pink City, on days 8 through 10. Take a trip to the Hawa Mahal, City Palace, and Amber Fort. The Jawahar Circle and Nahargarh Fort are great places to get a taste of the local culture.

If you want to see the Ganges River, go to Varanasi between November 11 and November 14. Stop by the temples and ghats as you cruise down the river.

On days 15 through 17, take a trip to Khajuraho to see the city's famous artwork, sculptures, and temples.

Day 18–20: Board a train for Bangalore, where you can admire the gorgeous parks, gardens, and lakes. For a chance to experience the area's rich natural beauty, go to the nearby Nandi Hills.

From Day 21 through Day 23, take a trip to Goa, where you can unwind on the beaches and admire the architecture with Portuguese influences.

Days 24 through 27 are dedicated to a trip to Mysore where you can explore the city's palaces and gardens.

Go backwater cruising and explore Kerala on the 28th and 30th day. For a breathtaking view of the coconut trees lining the canals, take a boat ride.

Return to Delhi on the thirty-first day to catch your journey home.
India is a wonderful destination because of the variety of its cultures, landscapes, and climes. No matter if a traveler is seeking a spiritual trip, an opportunity to explore a different culture, or a relaxing holiday, India has something to offer them. You have the opportunity to spend a month completely immersed in India's sights, sounds, and culture while creating precious memories.

India on a Budget

India's budget is an annual document presented by the Finance Minister in the Parliament which outlines the spending and revenue plans of the government for the upcoming financial year. The budget is divided into two parts – the Revenue Budget and the Capital Budget. The Revenue Budget includes government receipts and expenditure related to non-developmental activities, while the Capital Budget includes government's spending on infrastructure and developmental activities.

Revenue Budget:

The Revenue Budget of India includes all revenues received by the government from taxes, non-tax revenues and other sources. It also includes all expenditure incurred by the government on running its administration, defense, subsidies, and other non-developmental activities.

Tax Revenues:

India's major tax revenues come from the direct taxes, such as income tax, corporate tax, wealth tax, property tax, etc. and indirect taxes, such as customs and excise duties, service tax, etc.

Non-Tax Revenues:

Non-tax revenues of the government include receipts from government departments, earnings from public sector enterprises and disinvestment of government's stake in public sector enterprises.

Other Sources:

The other sources of revenue for the government include grants from international organizations, external borrowings, and public sector borrowing.

Expenditure:

The government expenditure includes salary and wages, pensions, interest payments, and subsidies.

Capital Budget:
The Capital Budget includes government expenditure on the purchase of assets such as land, buildings, machinery, equipment, and investments in shares. It also includes loans taken by the government to finance its developmental activities.

Capital Receipts:
The capital receipts of the government include external borrowings, market borrowings, and disinvestment of government's stake in public sector enterprises.

Expenditure:
The capital expenditure of the government includes expenditure on infrastructure such as roads, bridges, railways, irrigation and power projects, etc., and expenditure on social sector schemes such as education, health, employment, etc.

India's budget plays a key role in driving the country's economic growth as it outlines the government's priorities for the year. It is important for citizens to understand the budget and its implications for their lives, so that they can hold the government accountable for its expenditure.

Special Interest Tours

India is a country of contrasts and vibrant cultures, and it offers a range of specialized and interesting tours for visitors who are looking for something a little more unique. From wildlife safaris and mountain treks to spiritual pilgrimages and local cuisine tours, there is something to suit every type of traveler. Here is a list of some of the most popular specialized tours in India:

1. Wildlife Safari: India is home to some of the world's most iconic wildlife species such as tigers, elephants, and leopards. Wildlife safaris offer a unique opportunity to get close to these majestic creatures in their natural habitat. You can choose to explore the forests of the famous national parks like Ranthambore or Kaziranga or opt for a private safari in the lesser-known reserves like Bandhavgarh and Corbett.

2. Mountain Trekking: India's Himalayan range offers some of the best trekking opportunities in the world. From the classic round of the Annapurna Circuit in Nepal to the challenging trek to the summit of Mount Everest, there is something for everyone. If you're a beginner, why not try the moderate treks in Himachal Pradesh or the Garhwal region of Uttarakhand.

3. Spiritual Pilgrimages: India is the birthplace of many religions and spiritual paths, and it is a great destination for many spiritual seekers. Popular pilgrimage sites include the Golden Temple in Amritsar, the Taj Mahal in Agra, and the Vaishno Devi Shrine in Jammu.

4. Cultural Tours: India is a land of diverse cultures, and a cultural tour is a great way to explore the country's many traditions. Popular cultural tours include the Golden Triangle in North India, the temples of South India, and the desert cities of Rajasthan.

5. Culinary Tours: India is known for its delicious cuisine, and a culinary tour is the perfect way to explore the country's gastronomic delights. Popular culinary tours include the Delhi Food Tour, the Mumbai Street Food Tour, and the Chennai Coastal Food Tour.

6. Adventure Tours: India is a great destination for thrill-seekers, and there are plenty of adventure tours available. From white-water rafting in Rishikesh to paragliding in Manali, you can find a wide range of exciting activities to choose from.
India is a vast and varied country with a range of specialized and interesting tours to offer. Whether you're looking for a wildlife safari, a spiritual pilgrimage, or a culinary tour, India has something for everyone. So, why not start exploring the country and discover its many wonders?

Spiritual India

India is a land of spirituality and religion, and has long been known as a spiritual destination for those seeking enlightenment and inner peace. From ancient times, people have journeyed to India to experience its spiritual culture, to learn its ancient wisdom and to explore its many religions.

The spiritual India includes many different spiritual traditions and practices. The most popular and widely recognized are Hinduism, Buddhism, Jainism, and Sikhism. Each of these religions has its own unique beliefs and customs, and many of them are still practiced today.

Hinduism is the oldest and largest religion in India, and its beliefs and practices have had a major influence on other religions in the region. Hinduism is based on the Vedas, ancient texts that form the basis of the religion. Hindus believe in the cycle of birth, death, and rebirth, and the ultimate goal of life is to attain moksha, or liberation from the cycle of rebirth. Hinduism has a variety of gods, goddesses, and spiritual practices, such as yoga and meditation, which are used to help achieve enlightenment. Buddhism is another major religion in India, and it is based on the teachings of the Buddha. Buddhists believe in the Four Noble Truths and the Eightfold Path, which are designed to help people lead a more meaningful and spiritual life.

Buddhism is also known for its peaceful practices such as meditation and mindfulness, which allow people to gain insight into their inner selves.

Jainism is an ancient religion that originated in India and is based on the teachings of the Jain saints. Jains believe in non-violence and respect for all living things, and their spiritual practices involve meditation, fasting, and pilgrimage.

Sikhism is a religion that originated in India and is based on the teachings of the Sikh Gurus. Sikhs believe in the principle of Ik Onkar, the Oneness of God, and the practice of living a life of service to others. They also practice meditation and other spiritual disciplines to help them reach a higher state of consciousness.

India has also been a center of spiritual practices such as yoga and ayurveda, both of which have been used for centuries to promote health and well-being. Yoga is an ancient practice that combines physical postures, breathing exercises, and meditation to promote health and relaxation. Ayurveda is an ancient healing system that uses herbal remedies and other natural treatments to promote health and balance within the body.

Spiritual India is a land of mystery, beauty, and enlightenment. It is a place where people can explore their inner self, learn ancient wisdom, and experience the power of spirituality. Whether you are looking for a spiritual retreat, a meditation retreat, or simply a place to find inner peace, India is the place to go.

Cultural India

India is a country of immense cultural diversity, with a rich and vibrant heritage. From the ancient Indus Valley civilization to the present day, Indian culture has been shaped by a variety of influences, including its geography, religious beliefs, and the impact of foreign invaders. India is a melting pot of cultures and traditions, making it one of the world's most fascinating countries.

Whether you're looking to explore the vibrant sights and sounds of India's many festivals or to experience its unique cuisine, there is something for everyone to enjoy. Here's a list of some of India's most popular cultural attractions:

1. Festivals: India hosts a wide variety of festivals throughout the year, from the colorful Holi festival to the Kumbh Mela and Diwali. These festivals provide a unique insight into the diversity of India's people and culture and are an essential part of the country's cultural heritage.

2. Cuisine: Indian cuisine is renowned for its use of spices and flavors. From the fragrant biryani to the tangy tandoori, Indian food has something for everyone.

3. Arts and Crafts: Indian art and craft is renowned for its intricate detail and vibrant colors. From painting to sculpture, Indian art is a reflection of the country's rich cultural heritage.

4. Dance and Music: India's dance and music is a reflection of its diverse cultural background. From classical forms such as Bharatanatyam to modern genres like Bollywood, India's dance and music provide a window into its soul.

5. Architecture: India's architecture is a blend of Hindu, Islamic, and European influences. From the famed Taj Mahal to the ancient temples of Khajuraho, India's architectural heritage is a testament to its cultural history.

6. Religion: India is home to many of the world's major religions, including Hinduism, Buddhism, Jainism, and Sikhism. Religion plays an integral role in India's culture and is reflected in its art, literature, and architecture.

7. Textiles and Clothing: Indian textiles and clothing are renowned for their bright colors and intricate patterns. From saris to sherwanis, India's traditional clothing is a reflection of its culture and heritage.

India's culture is truly unique and varied, with something to offer everyone. From its vibrant festivals to its timeless art and architecture, India is a country with a rich and varied cultural heritage.

No matter where you go in India, you will find something to enjoy. From its beautiful beaches to its majestic mountains, India has something for everyone. Whether you're interested in exploring the country's natural beauty or its vibrant cities, you'll find plenty to explore. From its vibrant street markets to its ancient monuments, India is a country that offers a wealth of cultural attractions. From its rich cuisine to its vibrant religious ceremonies, India is a country where you'll never run out of things to do. From its ancient art forms to its modern-day entertainment, India has something for everyone. India is a country that is vibrant, diverse, and full of life, and its culture is something that should be experienced by everyone.

Adventure India

India is a land of incredible beauty, with diverse cultures and landscapes that offer plenty of exciting adventure opportunities. Whether you're looking for an extreme adventure or a more leisurely experience, India has something to offer everyone. From snow-capped mountains to lush jungles and beautiful beaches, India is an adventure-seeker's paradise. Here are some of the top adventure activities to explore in India:

1. Trekking:
India has some of the most spectacular mountain ranges in the world, making it an ideal destination for trekking. The Himalayas, the Western Ghats, the Karakoram and the Aravalli are some of the most popular trekking destinations in India.

Trekking in India can be a great way to experience the beauty of the country and its culture.

2. White Water Rafting:

White water rafting is a thrilling way to explore the rivers of India. From the Ganges in the north to the Brahmaputra in the east and the Godavari in the south, India offers plenty of white water rafting opportunities.

3. Skiing:

India is home to some of the best ski resorts in the world, offering plenty of opportunities for skiing. The Himalayan Mountains, the Nilgiris and the Aravalli offer some of the best skiing in India.

4. Mountaineering:

Mountaineering in India is an excellent way to explore the vast and varied landscape of the country. With some of the highest peaks in the world, India offers plenty of mountaineering opportunities. The Himalayan Mountains are the most popular destination for mountaineering.

5. Rock Climbing:

Rock climbing is a popular adventure activity in India, with plenty of opportunities for climbers of all levels. India has some of the best rock climbing spots in the world, from the granite cliffs of the Western Ghats to the sandstone cliffs of the Himalayas.

6. Paragliding:

Paragliding in India is a great way to experience the beauty of the country from the skies. The Himalayan Mountains, the Western Ghats, the Eastern Ghats and the Aravalli offer some of the best paragliding sites in India.

7. Bungee Jumping:

Bungee jumping is an adrenaline-pumping adventure activity, and India has some of the best bungee jumping sites in the world. From the Andaman Islands to the Western Ghats, India offers plenty of bungee jumping opportunities.

8. Caving:

Caving is another popular adventure activity in India. With its vast network of caves, India offers plenty of caving opportunities. The Western Ghats and the Himalayas are the most popular caving destinations in India.

Whether you're looking for an extreme adventure or a leisurely experience, India has something to offer everyone. With its diverse geography and culture, India is an ideal destination for adventure enthusiasts. So make sure to explore the adventure opportunities that India has to offer!

Indian's principle

India is a diverse country with a variety of cultures, religions, beliefs, and customs. Over the years, it has developed its own set of principles and beliefs that guide its citizens and shape its society. These principles are influenced by a rich history and the values of our nation. Here is a list of some of the most important principles of India.

1. Unity in Diversity:
India is a land of many cultures, religions, languages and beliefs. This rich diversity is celebrated and integrated into the national identity. We strive to promote unity and harmony among different communities and celebrate our differences as strengths.

2. Respect for All:
In India, respect for all is paramount. People from all walks of life are respected and given equal rights and opportunities, regardless of caste, religion, gender, or economic status.

3. Non-Violence:
Non-violence is a core principle of India. The nation has a long history of peaceful protests and civil disobedience as a means to achieve social and political change.

4. Compassion:

Compassion and kindness are deeply ingrained in Indian culture. People are encouraged to help those in need and care for the environment and animals.

5. Community:
India places a great emphasis on community and collective responsibility. People are encouraged to prioritize the needs of the community over their own and work together for the common good.

6. Education:
Education is highly valued in India and is seen as a path to a brighter future. People are encouraged to pursue their studies and gain knowledge and skills to contribute to society.

7. Spirituality:
India is a spiritual nation and many people practice yoga, meditation, and other spiritual practices to find peace and a sense of purpose.

8. Patriotism:
Patriotism is an important principle in India. People are proud of their nation's history and its achievements and strive to make India a better place.

9. Equality:

India is a land where all citizens are equal and have the same rights and opportunities. We strive to create a society where everyone is treated with respect and dignity and no one is discriminated against.

10. Environmentalism:

India is a country with a rich natural heritage and we are committed to preserving it for future generations. We promote environmental sustainability and advocate for the protection of our forests, rivers, and wildlife.

11. Tolerance:

Tolerance is an important principle in India. We strive to create a society where everyone is accepted and respected, regardless of their beliefs or backgrounds.

12. Family:

Family is an integral part of Indian culture and a strong bond of love and loyalty binds families together. People strive to create a supportive and nurturing environment for their family members.

13. Self-Reliance:

Self-reliance is an important principle in India. People are encouraged to use their skills and talents to become financially independent and contribute to society.

14. Service:

Service is a core value in India. People are encouraged to serve others and use their talents to create a better society.

15. Integrity:
Integrity is a core principle of India. We strive to create a society where all citizens are honest, responsible, and accountable for their actions.

These principles are the foundation of Indian society and help shape the culture and values of our nation. It is important to remember them and use them to build a better future for India.

Indian's Principles of Management

Indian Principles of Management India has a long history of management, with ancient principles and practices that can still be seen in many businesses today. The Indian principles of management are based on the idea of managing people and resources to achieve organizational goals. These principles have been adapted and modified over the years to meet the changing needs of organizations.

1. Dharma: Dharma is the idea of having a moral code of ethics to guide all activities. It emphasizes the importance of doing right and avoiding wrong.

Dharma is the basis for trust and loyalty among employees.

2. Karma: Karma is the concept of cause and effect, wherein good deeds are rewarded while bad deeds are punished. It is believed that if an individual performs good deeds, they will be blessed with success.

3. Adhikara: Adhikara is the principle of authority, which states that authority should be used for the benefit of the organization. It is based on the idea that each person should be given the opportunity to contribute to the success of the organization.

4. Swadhyaya: Swadhyaya is the concept of self-learning, which encourages employees to be proactive in their development. It stresses the importance of self-improvement and encourages employees to take initiative in their own development.

5. Ahimsa: Ahimsa is the principle of non-violence and is based on the idea that all people should be treated with respect. It stresses the importance of a peaceful environment in the workplace and encourages employees to resolve conflicts peacefully.

6. Satya: Satya is the concept of truth and honesty. It emphasizes the importance of being honest and truthful in all interactions with others.

7. Asatya: Asatya is the principle of non-deception. It stresses the importance of not deceiving others in order to achieve organizational goals.

8. Loka Samastha: Loka Samastha is the concept of collective responsibility. It is based on the idea that all members of the organization should be held accountable for the success or failure of the organization.

9. Vasudhaiva Kutumbakam: Vasudhaiva Kutumbakam is the principle of global responsibility. It encourages employees to think beyond their immediate environment and take into account the larger global community.

10. Vasudhaiva Kutumbakam: Vasudhaiva Kutumbakam is the principle of global responsibility. It encourages employees to think beyond their immediate environment and take into account the larger global community. The Indian principles of management have been adapted and modified over the years to meet the changing needs of organizations. By understanding and following these principles, organizations can ensure that their employees are engaged, motivated, and productive. By following these principles, organizations can also create an environment that is conducive to growth and innovation.

Authenticity and Nightlife

Authenticity and nightlife in India are two concepts that go hand in hand. India is a country that has a wide variety of cultures and customs that make it unique. As such, its nightlife can be both traditional and modern. Some of the most authentic forms of nightlife in India include street food parties, rooftop dinners, and open-air bars. Street food parties are especially popular in major cities like Mumbai, Bangalore, and Delhi. Street food stands serve up a unique blend of Indian and global cuisines, such as vegetarian and non-vegetarian dishes. In addition, many of these stands also feature live performances from local artists. Rooftop dinners are also a popular form of nightlife in India. These dinners are often held in high-rise buildings and feature a wide variety of dishes from all over India.

Open-air bars are also popular in India. These bars often feature live music, DJs, and traditional Indian dancing. They offer a unique atmosphere and provide an opportunity to mingle with locals and tourists alike. Nightclubs are also a popular form of nightlife in India. These nightclubs often feature international and local DJs, as well as live music. In addition, many of these clubs also offer a variety of food and beverages, making them the perfect place to enjoy an evening out. Finally, India is home to some of the world's most incredible festivals. From the Kumbh Mela to the Holi Festival, India's festivals are a great way to experience the culture and the people of India. Many of these festivals also feature traditional music and dancing, as well as plenty of food and drinks. In conclusion, authenticity and nightlife in India are two concepts that go hand in hand. From street food parties to rooftop dinners, open-air bars to nightclubs, India offers a wide variety of nightlife experiences that are both traditional and modern. Additionally, India's festivals are a great way to experience the culture and the people of India.

Chapter 7: Travelling Essentials.

With the beauty and diversity of India, it is no surprise that so many people are drawn to the country for travel. Whether you are visiting for a few days or longer, there are some vital travel essentials that you should bring with you in order to make your journey more comfortable and enjoyable.

1. Passport and Visa: Depending on your nationality, you may need a visa to enter India. Make sure to check the visa requirements and apply for a visa if necessary. You should also bring your passport with you at all times.

2. Money: India's currency is the Indian Rupee (INR). It is a good idea to exchange some money before you arrive in India so that you can have some cash on hand. You can also use credit cards and debit cards at many places, but it is best to have some cash on hand just in case.

3. Clothing: Depending on the time of year and your destination, you should pack clothing accordingly. If you are visiting during the summer months, light, breathable clothing is recommended. In wintertime, make sure to bring warm clothes and a raincoat or umbrella in case it rains.

4. Travel Insurance: It is always a good idea to purchase travel insurance before you leave for your trip. This will help cover any medical expenses, lost luggage, or other unexpected costs that may occur while you are away.

5. Phone and Internet: India has a good mobile network, so it is a good idea to buy a local SIM card for your phone. This will allow you to make calls and access the internet while you are in the country.

6. Maps and Guidebooks: Having a good guidebook or map of your destination will help you get around and find the best places to visit. Make sure to buy one before you leave for your trip so that you can plan your route accordingly.

7. Sunscreen and Insect Repellent: India can get quite hot during the summer, so it is important to bring sunscreen to protect your skin from the sun. You should also bring an insect repellent to ward off any pesky bugs.

8. First Aid Kit: Having a small first aid kit with you can be very useful in case of any minor cuts, scrapes, or other injuries. Make sure to include items such as bandages, antiseptic ointment, painkillers, and anything else you might need.
With these essentials in hand, you can have a safe and comfortable journey through India. Whether

you are visiting for a few days or longer, these items will help ensure that your trip is an enjoyable and memorable one.

What to Pack for India

When planning a trip to India, it is important to make sure you have all the essentials in your luggage. From clothing and toiletries to electronics, here is a list of what to pack for India.

Clothing:
• Lightweight, breathable fabrics such as cotton and linen are recommended for hot weather. Pack a variety of tops and bottoms, including a few long sleeve shirts and long pants for cooler evenings.
• Bring comfortable walking shoes, sandals or flip-flops, and a hat or scarf to protect from the sun.
• A light jacket or wrap may be helpful if you plan to visit the mountains.
• Modest clothing is recommended for most places in India, especially for women.

Toiletries:
• For hygiene purposes, it is best to pack your own toiletries.
• Sunscreen and insect repellent are essential.
• A first-aid kit is also recommended, including pain relievers, anti-diarrhea medication, and anti-vomiting medication.

• A sleeping mask and ear plugs can be useful on long train rides.
• Don't forget your brush, toothpaste, and any other toiletries you need.

Electronics:

• A universal adapter is a must for charging any electronic devices you bring.
• A cell phone with international roaming is helpful, but it is also a good idea to bring a few prepaid SIM cards for local use.
• A small laptop or tablet may be useful for work or entertainment.
• An external hard drive is also recommended for backing up data.

Other Items:

• Pack a small day bag for sightseeing.
• A flashlight can be useful for power outages.
• A water bottle with a filter can be a lifesaver.
•Endeavour to come along with few books and magazines
• A journal or notebook can be a great way to document your trip.
• A small amount of cash in local currency is also essential.

By packing the right items, you can make sure you have a comfortable and enjoyable trip to India.

What to Expect from the Weather

India is a large country with different climates, and its downfall can be changeable. Depending on where you are in India, you can anticipate to substantiation a range of climates and downfall patterns. The northern part of India has a cool, temperate climate and is one of the most temperate corridor of the country. During the time-out months, temperatures can drop to 0 °C or below, and during the summer, temperatures can reach up to 40 °C or advanced. downfall is fairly harmonious throughout the time. The central part of India has a tropical climate, with hot and sticky downfall during the summer months, from April to June. Temperatures generally range from 20 °C to 40 °C. Rainstorm season generally runs from late June until September, bringing heavy rain and showers. The southern part of India has a tropical climate as well, with temperatures ranging from 20 °C to 35 °C. downfall is generally more harmonious than in the northern and central corridor of the country, with the rainstorm season generally lasting from October to December. Overall, India gests a range of climates, from temperate in the north to tropical in the south. downfall is generally harmonious throughout the country, but during the summer months, heavy rain and showers can be anticipated in certain areas. No matter where you are in the country, it's important to be prepared for unlooked-for changes in the downfall.

What to Do if You Get Sick

If you get sick in India, it is important to take the necessary precautions to ensure a speedy recovery. Here are some tips on what to do if you get sick in India:

1. Visit your local doctor: If you start to feel unwell, it is best to visit your local doctor or hospital as soon as possible. India has a wide range of medical facilities, from private hospitals and clinics to government-run health centers. Ensure to carry your health insurance documents, if you have any.

2. Follow doctor's advice: Make sure to follow the doctor's advice to the letter. If you are prescribed medication or need to take specific tests, ensure that you take the necessary steps to ensure your health and safety.

3. Stay hydrated: Dehydration is a common problem in India, especially during the hot summer months. Make sure to drink plenty of water throughout the day, and avoid sugary and caffeinated drinks.

4. Eat nutritious food: Eating a balanced diet is essential for staying healthy in India. Make sure to include plenty of fruits, vegetables, and proteins in your diet to keep your energy levels up.

5. Get rest: Make sure to get enough rest and sleep to ensure that your body has enough time to recover.

6. Seek help: If your illness is serious or persistent, seek help from a medical professional. In India, there are a range of helplines and services available to assist you.

7. Stay positive: It is important to stay positive and optimistic during your recovery. Make sure to keep in touch with friends and family, and find ways to de-stress and relax.

8. Practice good hygiene: Practicing proper hygiene is essential for staying healthy. Make sure to wash your hands regularly and avoid touching your face, eyes, and nose.

9. Avoid smoking and alcohol: Smokers and drinkers are more likely to pick up illnesses, so it is important to avoid these activities while you are ill.

10. Wear protective clothing: In India, the weather can be harsh. Make sure to dress appropriately for the climate and wear protective clothing such as hats, sunglasses, and sunscreen.

11. Take preventive measures: If you are traveling to India, make sure to take preventive measures to protect yourself from illnesses, such as getting vaccinated and taking preventive medications.

12. Seek alternative treatments: If you are looking for alternative treatments, there are a range of traditional and natural remedies available in India. However, make sure to consult a qualified medical professional before taking any of these treatments.

Following these steps should help you to stay healthy and safe if you get sick in India. Remember to always seek medical advice if you're feeling unwell, and take the necessary steps to ensure your health and safety.

Tips and Advice

India is a vast and diverse country with a captivating history, culture and customs. Tourists from around the world come to explore its vibrant cities, ancient monuments, and beautiful landscapes. However, there are some important tips and advice that visitors should keep in mind to ensure a safe and enjoyable trip.

1. Research Before You Go: Before visiting India, be sure to research the culture, customs, and laws of the country. Knowing about these things will help you navigate the country more easily and safely.

2. Be Aware of the Climate: India has an extremely varied climate, ranging from hot and humid in the south to cold and dry in the north. Make sure to pack the right clothing according to the region you are visiting.

3. Respect Local Customs: India is a conservative country, and it's important to be respectful of the local customs and traditions. Show respect by dressing modestly and avoiding public displays of affection.

4. Avoid Scams: India is known for its scams and hustles, so be alert and aware of any potential scams. Avoid giving money to anyone who promises something in return and always be sure to get a receipt.

5. Carry a Map: India can be quite confusing to navigate, so it's important to always have a map. A GPS device is also useful, but be sure to carry a paper map as a backup.

6. Learn Some Hindi: Knowing some basic Hindi words and phrases will help you communicate with locals. This will also make it easier to get around and make new friends.

7. Take Care of Your Health: India can be a challenging place to travel in terms of sanitation and hygiene. Be sure to drink only bottled or boiled water and take necessary precautions to avoid getting sick.

8. Use Public Transport: India has an extensive public transport system, and it is usually the most affordable option. Buses, trains, and auto-rickshaws are all available in most cities.

9. Get Travel Insurance: Travel insurance is essential for any trip to India. Make sure to get a comprehensive policy that covers medical expenses, trip cancellation, and other potential risks.

10. Have Fun: India is an incredible country with so much to explore and experience. Make sure to take time to enjoy all the sights and sounds of this amazing country!

India Solo Travelers

India has become home to a growing number of solo travelers. From backpackers and digital nomads to retirees and business travelers, more and more people are exploring India on their own. Whether it's the exotic culture, breathtaking landscapes or the friendly locals, India offers something for every type of solo traveler. Below are some of the key points to consider when planning a solo trip to India:

1. Choose your destination wisely: India is a vast country with a wide range of climates, cultures and attractions. When planning your trip, consider the places you want to visit, the type of activities you'd like to do, and the kind of people you want to meet. This will help you narrow down your destination choices and ensure you get the most out of your India adventure.

2. Prepare for the culture shock: India is a very different cultural and social environment from what most Westerners are used to. Be prepared for some culture shock and be sure to research the customs and cultural norms of the areas you'll be visiting.

3. Research safety precautions: India is generally a safe country, but it's important to take common-sense safety precautions when traveling alone. Research the areas you'll be visiting, plan ahead and be aware of your surroundings.

4. Take advantage of local resources: Local tourist offices and travel agents can be a great resource for solo travelers. They can help you find accommodation, provide advice on what to see and do and even recommend trustworthy local guides.

5. Stay connected: Make sure you have an international phone plan, a reliable Wi-Fi connection and an extra battery pack. This will help you stay connected with family and friends back home and make it easier to contact local resources if needed.

6. Have fun: India is an amazing country with plenty of things to see and do. So don't forget to enjoy yourself. Whether it's a yoga class in the foothills of the Himalayas or a cooking class in a local village, there's something for everyone.
Solo travel can be a great way to explore a new country, and India is no exception. By researching your destination and taking common-sense safety precautions, you can have a safe and rewarding experience. So get packing and enjoy all that India has to offer.

Helpful India phrases

India is a vibrant and diverse country with its own unique culture, language and customs. As a result, it can be difficult to get to grips with the language and customs of India if you are not a native speaker. To help you get the most out of your stay in India, here is a list of helpful India phrases that will help you to communicate more effectively and make your trip even more enjoyable:

1. Namaste: This is one of the most common greetings in India and translates to 'hello'. It is a respectful way to greet someone, and is usually accompanied by a slight bow and hands pressed together in prayer position.

2. Dhanyavaad: This phrase is used to express gratitude and thank someone for their help. It translates to 'thank you'.

3. Shukriyaa: Another way to express gratitude, 'shukriyaa' translates to 'thank you very much'.

4. Aapka swagat hai: This phrase translates to 'welcome' and is used to greet someone in a friendly, hospitable manner.

5. Kripyaa: This phrase is used to ask for help or assistance, and translates to 'please'.

6. Maaf kijiye: This phrase is used to politely apologise for something, and translates to 'I'm sorry'.

7. Kya aap hindi bolte hain?: This phrase is used to ask if someone speaks Hindi, and translates to 'Do you speak Hindi?'

8. Main thoda samajh nahi paya: This phrase is used to politely let someone know that you don't understand what they are saying, and translates to 'I didn't understand'.

9. Aapko mera salaam: This phrase is used to express respect and good wishes to someone, and translates to 'Greetings to you'.

10. Aap kuch samajhte hain?: This phrase is used to ask if someone understands what is being said, and translates to 'Do you understand?'

11. Kya aap mujhe bata sakte hain?: This phrase is used to ask someone to explain something, and translates to 'Can you tell me?'

12. Main aapko bahut shukriyaa karta hun: This phrase is used to express sincere gratitude, and translates to 'I am very grateful to you'.

13. Kya aap mujhe sahara de sakte hain?: This phrase is used to ask for help or assistance, and translates to 'Can you help me?'

14. Aap Ka dhanyavad: This phrase is used to express sincere thanks, and translates to 'Thank you very much'.

15. Main aapko samajh nahi paaya: This phrase is used to politely let someone know that you didn't understand what they said, and translates to 'I didn't understand you'.

16. Please aap mujhe samjha de: This phrase is used to ask someone to explain something, and translates to 'Please explain to me'.

17. Main aapko maaf karta hun: This phrase is used to apologize for something, and translates to 'I apologize to you'.

18. Main aapkaa bahut shukriyaa karta hun: This phrase is used to express sincere gratitude, and translates to 'I am very grateful to you'.

19. Aapkaa dhanyavaad bahut adhik: This phrase is used to express sincere thanks, and translates to 'Thank you very much'.

20. Aapka swagat hai: This phrase is used to welcome someone, and translates to 'Welcome'.
By familiarizing yourself with these useful India phrases, you can make the most of your visit to India and ensure that you have a pleasant and successful trip.

Fun Facts about India

1. India is the world's largest democracy and the second most populous country in the world.

2. India is home to the world's largest movie industry, known as Bollywood.

3. India is the birthplace of Buddhism and one of the most ancient civilizations in the world.

4. India is home to seven World Heritage Sites and more than 100 National Parks.

5. India is the world's second largest English speaking country after the United States.

6. India is the world's largest producer of milk, tea and jute.

7. India has the world's largest postal system with over 150,000 post offices.

8. India is the world's third largest economy and home to the world's biggest IT services sector.

9. India has the world's third largest army and the world's largest volunteer army.

10. India is the world's largest producer of mangoes and the world's second largest producer of bananas.

11. India is the world's fourth largest producer of automobiles and the world's fifth largest producer of commercial vehicles.

12. India is the world's second largest producer of cotton and the world's third largest producer of silk.

13. India is the world's sixth largest producer of wheat and the world's seventh largest producer of rice.

14. India is the world's largest producer of spices and the world's second largest producer of tobacco.

15. India is the world's second largest producer of sugarcane and the world's third largest producer of coffee.

16. India is the world's fifth largest producer of vegetables and the world's sixth largest producer of fruits.

17. India is the world's largest consumer of gold and the world's second largest consumer of silver.

18. India is the world's largest importer of arms and the world's largest importer of nuclear technology.

19. India is home to the world's oldest living religion, Hinduism.

20. India is the birthplace of Yoga, Ayurveda, and many other traditional healing practices.

21. India is the world's oldest and most diverse culture, with a rich heritage and diverse religions.

22. India is home to the world's tallest mountain range, the Himalayas.

23. India is the world's seventh largest country, covering an area of 3,287,263 km2.

24. India has the world's longest coastline, stretching over 7500 km.

25. India is the world's second most populous country, with over 1.3 billion people.

Printed in Great Britain
by Amazon

23917030R00119